# We Made a Garden

# We Made a Garden

Margery Fish

BATSFORD

First published in the United Kingdom
in 1956 by W. H. and L. Collingridge Limited.

This edition first published in the United Kingdom in 2023 by
Batsford
43 Great Ormond Street
London
WC1N 3HZ

An imprint of B. T. Batsford Holdings Limited

ISBN 978 1 84994 872 2

A CIP catalogue record for this book is available from the British Library.

10 9 8 7 6 5 4 3 2 1

Reproduction by Rival Colour Ltd, UK
Printed and bound by Toppan Leefung Ltd, China

This book can be ordered direct from the publisher at
www.batsfordbooks.com, or try your local bookshop

# Contents

# Foreword

This is the book which started it all for Margery Fish and for gardeners around the world for whom she and her garden have been such an inspiration. As war approached in the late 1930s Margery and her husband Walter bought a house out of London, East Lambrook Manor in Somerset, and set about restoring the house and making a garden. This book is an account of their adventure.

For the first few years that they lived at East Lambrook, they divided their time between Somerset and London – Walter was editor of the *Daily Mail* and Margery had been assistant to Lord Northcliffe, its proprietor. Clearly, the garden had to be easy to look after; they both also believed that it should be in harmony with the stone house, and they wanted it to be presentable all the year round. These ideas inspired both her gardening style and her writing; and through this book, the seven others and her many magazine articles she brought her influential ideas to a wide audience.

Margery and Walter were very different characters. One of the recurrent themes of *We Made a Garden* (originally proposed under the not very catchy title of *Gardening with Walter*) is the uneasy horticultural relationship between the two – Walter preferred bold and colourful plants and fought a not always good-humoured battle with his wife to ensure prominence for his dahlias. Margery, who hated dahlias, was more interested in primroses, double daisies, hellebores and other less brash varieties. But their devotion to each other transcended such differences of taste in spite of Walter's sometimes thoughtless disregard for her favourites – which she herself lovingly recounts here.

At first she tells Walter his beloved dahlias are 'only fit for a circus'; later, as his strength deserted him, she planted his dahlias for him even though she was also secretly relieved when they failed to survive their winter in storage; then, after he died, she took pleasure in seeing the few remaining varieties coming up year after year. The book is an account of their relationship, as the original title indicated, as well as the garden.

Since Margery Fish died in 1969 her garden has enjoyed mixed fortunes but in recent years has been restored, looked after carefully and is open to visitors daily for much of the year. Margery's nursery, through which she disseminated such a variety of choice plants, is again flourishing, and varieties which she herself discovered and introduced to gardeners are again being made more widely available. Her evocative and infectious writing style, coupled with her astute observation of the plants themselves, has long inspired gardeners and continues to do so. She helped make our gardens the way they are.

*Graham Rice, 2002*

# Introduction

When, in 1937, my husband decided there was a likelihood of war, and we made up our minds to buy a house in the country, all our friends thought we'd choose a respectable house in good repair complete with garden, all nicely laid out and ready to walk into.

And when, instead, we chose a poor battered old house that had to be gutted to be livable, and a wilderness instead of a garden, they were really sorry for us. They were particularly sympathetic about the garden. Redoing a house could be fun, but how would two Londoners go about the job of creating a garden from a farmyard and a rubbish heap?

I have never regretted our foolhardiness. Of course, we made mistakes, endless mistakes, but at least they were our own, just as the garden was our own. However imperfect the result there is a certain satisfaction in making a garden that is like no one else's, and in knowing that you yourself are responsible for every stone and every flower in the place. It is pleasant to know each one of your plants intimately because you have chosen and planted every one of them. In course of time they become real friends, conjuring up pleasant associations of the people who gave them and the gardens they came from.

Walter and I had several things particularly in mind when we made the garden.

The first was that it must be as modest and unpretentious as the house, a cottage garden in fact, with crooked paths and unexpected corners.

Next it must be easy to run. When we bought the house we were living in London, and for the first two years we divided our time between London and Somerset, so our garden had to take care of itself for much of the time. We designed it with the idea that we'd have to look after it ourselves, and though there have been times when we had regular help they were brief and uncertain, and we knew we'd soon be back where so many people are today, depending on a little casual labour when we can get it.

Since Walter died I have had to simplify it even more, as the garden can only have the odd hours that are left over in a busy life. He made me realize that the aim of all gardeners should be a garden that is always presentable – not a Ruth Draperish garden that has been, or will be, but never is at its best. We don't apologize for our homes because we keep them garnished regularly as a matter of course, and I have never understood why we don't feel exactly the same about a garden.

Another thing he taught me was that you mustn't rely on your flowers to make your garden attractive. A good bone structure must come first, with an intelligent use of evergreen plants so that the garden is always clothed, no matter what time of year. Flowers are an added delight, but a good garden is the garden you enjoy looking at even in the depths of winter. There ought never to be a moment when it is not pleasant and interesting. To achieve this means a lot of thought and a lot of work, but it can be done.

# The House

The house was long and low, in the shape of an L, built of honey-coloured Somerset stone. At one time it must have been thatched but, unfortunately, that had been discarded long ago and old red tiles used instead. It stood right in the middle of a little Somerset village, and made the corner where a very minor road turned off from the main street. There was only a narrow strip of garden in front, and not very much behind, but we bought an orchard and outbuildings beyond so that we had about two acres in all. A high stone wall screened us from the village street, and there was a cottage and another orchard on the other side.

You can't make a garden in a hurry, particularly one belonging to an old house. House and garden must look as if they had grown up together and the only way to do this is to live in the house, get the feel of it, and then by degrees the idea of a garden will grow.

We didn't start work outside for nearly a year, and by that time we felt we belonged to the place and it belonged to us and we had some ideas of what we wanted to do with it.

It was on a warm September day when we first saw the house but it was such a wreck that Walter refused to go further than the hall, in spite of the great jutting chimney that buttressed the front. Then the long roof was patched with corrugated iron, the little front garden was a jungle of rusty old laurels and inside an overpowering smell of creosote, newly applied, fought with the dank, grave-like smell of an unlived in house. 'Full of dry rot,' said Walter, 'not at any price,' and turned on his heel.

For three months we tried to find what we wanted. We looked at cottages and villas, gaunt Victorian houses perched uneasily on hilltops, and snug little homes wedged in forgotten valleys. Some were too big and most too small, some hadn't enough garden and others too much. Some were too isolated, others so mixed up with other houses that privacy would have been impossible. We lost our way and had bitter arguments, but we did discover what we didn't want. I couldn't see Walter in a four-roomed cottage with a kitchen tacked on to one end and a bathroom at the other, and I had no intention of landing myself with a barn of a place that would require several servants to keep it clean.

We were still hunting in November when our way took us very near the old house so summarily dismissed in September, so we turned down the lane which said 'East Lambrook one mile', just to see what had happened during those three months.

Quite a lot had happened. The front garden had been cleared of its laurels and the house looked much better. Old tiles had replaced the corrugated iron on the roof, and inside the walls had been washed with cream and the woodwork with glossy paint.

It is one of those typical Somerset houses with a central passage and a door at each end, so very attractive to look at and so very draughty for living. That day we thought only of the artistic angle. It was late afternoon and the sun was nearly setting. Both doors were open and through them we caught a glimpse of a tree and a green background against the sunlight.

That day I got Walter further than the flagged passage, and we explored the old bakehouse, with its enormous inglenook and open fireplace, low beamed ceiling and stone floor, and a gay little parlour beyond. On the other side was another large room with stone floor and an even bigger fireplace, and at the far end a lovely room with wonderful panelling. We both knew that our search had ended, we had come home.

I cannot remember just what happened after that but I shall never forget the day when the surveyor came to make his report. It was one of those awful days in early winter of cold, penetrating rain. The house was dark and very cold, and the grave-like dankness was back, in spite of all the new paint and distemper. The surveyor, poor man, had just lost his wife, and was as depressed – naturally – as the weather. Nor shall I ever forget Walter's indignation with the report when it did come in. The house, while sound in wind and limb, was described as being of 'no character'. We didn't think then that it had anything but character, rather sinister perhaps, but definitely character. Since then I have discovered that the house has a kindly disposition; I never come home without feeling I am welcome.

Having got our house we then had to give it up again so that it could be made habitable. For many months it was in the hands of the builders and all we could do was to pay hurried visits to see how things were going, and turn our eyes from the derelict waste that was to be the garden. Sometimes I escaped from the consultations for brief moments and frenziedly pulled up groundsel for as long as I was allowed. Walter never wanted to stay a moment longer than business required and it worried me to go off and leave tracts of outsize groundsel going to seed with prodigal abandon. My few snatched efforts made very little impression on the wilderness, but they made me feel better.

It was late in the summer before we could get into the house, and some time after that before we were able to get down to the garden in earnest. All the time we were clearing and cleaning in odd moments, working our way through the tangle of brambles and laurels and elders, and thinking all the time what we would do with our little plot. We both knew that it had to be tackled as a whole with a definite design for the complete garden, and we were lucky in having plenty to do while our ideas smouldered and simmered.

# The Garden

The garden that went with the house was divided at the back into two tiny gardens, with walls and small plots of grass. We supposed that these went back to the time when the house had been two cottages.

In addition to the walls dividing the two little gardens at the back another wall divided us from the barton, and beneath all these walls someone had amused himself by making banks and sticking in stones vertically, like almonds on a trifle. We imagined the idea was a nice ready-made rock garden for us to play with. The first thing we did, when we really set out minds to the garden, was to remove all the walls and stones and pile them up for future use. They were quite a problem, those piles of stones, as they were moved from place to place as we dealt with the ground where they were piled. I could not see how we should ever use them all.

The high wall that screened us from the road was finished in typical Somerset style with stones set upright, one tall and then one short. I have never discovered the reason for these jagged walls and I don't think they are at all attractive. I asked my local builder and all he could suggest was that it made a nice finish. I can think of more attractive ways of solving the problem without such a lavish use of big stones.

There was great scope for planting between the stones and Walter suggested I could get busy on the top of the wall while we decided what to do with the rest of the garden. So I bought a few easy rock plants and sowed seed of valerian and alyssum, aubrietia and arabis to clothe those jagged rocks. The great heaps of stones were at that time right up against the wall and I had to clamber up them each time I planted anything, and later when I wanted to water my little family.

The watering was usually done after dinner, and those were the days when one donned a long dress and satin slippers for this social occasion – which one didn't have to cook. I can't think how I avoided turning an ankle as I had to clutch my skirt with one hand and use the other for the watering can while the stones rocked and tipped under my weight.

By degrees, of course, we got rid of all the stones. We gave away cartloads to anyone who would fetch them, mostly farmers who tipped them near farm gates to defeat the Somersetshire mud. We used up the best of them ourselves in time. We little realized in those days that as our schemes progressed we should buy far more than we ever had in the beginning.

Since those days I have had all the upright stones removed from the tops of our walls, and flat stones laid horizontally instead. I always thought the uneven finish very ugly and in times of stress when I have been casting round for more stones to finish some enterprise I have grudged so many large and even stones doing no good at all. Gone are all the little treasures from the top of the wall; instead clematises clamber about and climbing roses are trained over the top of the wall so that the world outside can enjoy the blooms as well. The rock plants, or descendants of them, are now growing in the wall itself. By tucking them into every available crack and crevice I can bring the wall to life long before the plants get going in the border below. Great cascades of white and lavender, yellow and pink prevent the wall from looking cold and bare in the early spring.

Having torn down all our little walls and obstructions so that we could visualize what the place looked like without them, our next job was to clear the barton – the yard in front of the outbuildings and between us and the orchard.

That job would have frightened most people, but not Walter. Anyone who knows anything about farming can imagine the piles of iron and rubbish that had accumulated during the years. We had bought the outbuildings, barton and orchard from a chicken farmer, so in addition to the farming legacies we had all the relics of the chicken era as well. And to add interest there were old beds, rusty oil stoves, ancient corsets, pots, pans, tins and china, bottles and glass jars, and some big lumps of stone which may at one time have been used for crushing grain.

A bonfire burned in the middle of that desolation for many weeks, until one day Walter announced that the time had come to level the ground for a proper drive into the malthouse, which we used as a garage. I was told I must find another place to burn the barrowloads of weeds and muck I collected every day. I can remember arguing, without result, that the place where the bonfire burned could be left while the rest of the barton was tackled. I think Walter was very wise in being so firm with me. The only way to get jobs done is to be ruthless and definite.

There was no rubbish collection in those days, which was undoubtedly the reason for the horrible collection of stuff we found. Small things, such as china, glass and tins, were collected by us in barrowloads and as a short cut Walter had holes dug in odd places and the stuff tipped into them. In the course of time, as I have put more land into cultivation I have run into quite a number of these caches, and have decided that it really does not pay to take short cuts. Luckily we now have a regular salvage collection and having retrieved the grisly mementoes they are banished for good and all.

Between the barton and orchard were two walls, and Walter suggested we could make quite attractive rock gardens against them and thus add colour and interest to the barton. It was only after I had given my enthusiastic agreement that I discovered he wanted some way of disposing of the bigger rubbish that couldn't be buried. So all the old oil stoves, bits of bedsteads, lumps of iron and rolls of wire netting were distributed against the walls, and the rest of the job was handed over to me.

Luckily we had a garden boy working for us then and he was allowed to help me cover the hardware with earth, and between us we ransacked the heaps of stones for the nicest looking specimens. Neither of us had ever done anything of the sort before but we constructed what we thought were two very fine gardens.

Soon after this visitors appeared one day. One of them was an expert gardener and she didn't get further than the first rock garden. I thought she was filled with admiration for our handiwork and was waiting for the applause. But I discovered she was trying to get up her courage to tell me that all the stones were put in at the wrong angle. Instead of tipping slightly inwards to make a good pocket of soil which would hold the rain, mine had an outward tilt so that the first really heavy shower would see a lot of the soil washed away and the water would run off what was left.

The stones had to remain as they were for several months, a monument to my ignorance, but one happy day a cousin with a genius for gardening visited us and remade the gardens for me. Although there is a distinct downward slope towards the gate he placed the stones to give the effect of level strata of outcrop, something I could never have dreamed of and have never ceased to admire. From the house the effect is a luxurious display of rock plants growing out of the wall.

I had very few real rock plants to begin with, and those that I had were very small, so the first season I kept up a succession of colourful effects with annuals. I do not know whether the soil was particularly good or as a beginner I took more trouble and followed instructions implicitly, or perhaps I was just lucky. Certainly I have never again grown such superlative *Phlox Drummondii*, dwarf antirrhinums, mignonette, zinnias, clarkia, godetia and candytuft, to mention only a few. For once, and once only, I achieved displays that really looked like the pictures on the packet, and I thought that it was all just too easy.

Not being an orthodox gardener I do not even now restrict myself to rock plants on these gardens, although I have quite a lot of them there. I like something a little more generous, so there are hyssops and ceratostigma, trailing potentillas and penstemon and, to give body a few dwarf shrubs, and against the wall such things as *Veronica Haageana*, coronilla, *Salvia Grahamii**  and *S. Greggii**, and fabiana.

It was Walter's idea to lay some flat stones in front of each of the rock gardens. He thought it would look more generous than having the gravel right up to the stones. To begin with they were only flat stones, but very soon I started planting between them and tried a few Dresden China daisies that had been given to me. The little daisies were an immediate success, because they enjoyed the cool root run between the stones, and I think found the ground that had been used for chickens produced a very rich diet. They increased so rapidly that it wasn't long before I had every crevice filled with them, and in the spring when they were in full bloom the effect was very good.

Walter never showed much enthusiasm for the smaller plants I cherished so lovingly but the daisies were an exception. He wanted them everywhere, bands on either side of the path, and later when we planted flowering trees I was asked to encircle them with daisies.

I am afraid the manurial legacy from the chickens must have disappeared long ago but the daisies continue to thrive, and I think it is because I divide them so frequently. I give away hundreds every year and I meet them in the gardens of all my friends. There is only one thing to remember when dealing with these little daisies and that is to make sure the birds don't uproot all the newly planted divisions. Nothing excites their curiosity or cupidity more, unless it is shallots. If I am doing a large area I find it saves a lot of time and casualties if I cotton them until they are firmly settled.

Having disposed of the rubbish we were at last able to consider the lay-out of the garden at the back of the house. We wanted it to be as simple as possible, as much grass as we could get and a generous drive to the old malthouse, which we were using as a garage. We had to leave enough room for a paved path from the house to the barton, and the rest of the level ground was to be taken up with a lawn that would stretch to the gate leading into the barton. We knew that the bigger the lawn the more spacious would be our garden. Just as a plain carpet pushes out the walls and makes a room bigger, so a wide stretch of uninterrupted grass gives a feeling of space and restfulness. Why, oh! why, will people cut up their lawns and fill them with horrid little beds? Usually the smaller the garden the more little beds are cut in the lawn making it smaller still. I can sympathize with the desire to grow more flowers, but one long bed grows just as many plants as a series of tiny ones, and avoids the restlessness and spottiness of small beds dotted about the lawn.

Walter was rabid on this subject and never ceased to exclaim at the foolishness of some of the people we knew. There was one garden in particular which we both liked when we first knew it. Then it was the rectory, and was just what a rectory garden should be. A wide flagged path led up to the house, turning at right angles to the gate. The rest of the garden was grassed, with fairly wide borders all round, under the high walls. The garden was not particularly well kept, nor were there very interesting plants growing in the borders, a good rector hasn't time for that, but it was adequate and pleasant and just the setting for village fêtes and summer meetings of the Mothers' Union.

In time it ceased to be used as a rectory and came on the market. The next owner left it as it was, probably from lack of interest. Then it changed hands again and the new owners felt they had to do something to improve it. We thought they could have achieved this by concentrating on what was there. They could have replanted those ample borders with better plants, and introduced interesting climbers on the walls, but they thought there were all sorts of things that ought to be in a garden, no matter what size. So they worked very hard to cut up that peaceful old garden with hedges. The lawn was cut in half, more beds were made along the new hedges, in one half trees were dotted about a small stone monument, and mean little narrow paths intersected it still more. On the other side little bits of rock garden cropped up from the grass, there was a pond and a weeping tree, more little bits of paving and more little beds. If ever a garden was ruined that one was, and the new owners spent their lives clipping hedges and cutting round the horrid little beds.

Another garden we knew was ruined for Walter because the paths were too narrow and completely out of proportion to everything else. He liked breadth and generosity and a feeling of spaciousness in the garden as well as the house, and the elimination of all unnecessary detail.

One of the things we tried to do was to make the garden as much part of the house as possible. It was easier for us than some people because we made the garden round the house, and the construction of the house helped. The big door in the hall, where we always sat, opens directly into the garden. The hall is paved with flagstones and we paved the garden outside, which is on the same level. It was difficult to tell where one ended and the other began, in point of fact a great deal of the garden usually came into the house with me, and attention was continually being drawn to the shoe scraper and door-mat! In the summer the garden door is open all the time and we are always in and out. The front garden we paved too, and as the only way to reach it is through the house or round the road there were more reprimands when I carried baskets of plants or weeds through the house. In the winter there is always a wood fire smouldering on the open hearth in the hall, and it makes a wonderful funeral pyre for dangerous weeds, and a convenient source of supply when potash or charcoal are required for garden operations.

# The Lawn

And so our lawn was taken right up to the high wall. I was grudgingly allowed a narrow bed in which to plant a few perennials and the climbers that were to clothe the wall, but I was warned that it was not to encroach too much on the precious green grass.

We were lucky in having one tree in the garden, a variegated sycamore. That was the tree we saw through the open door the day we decided to buy the house, and today it is the only thing that remains in the garden from those days. It is in the lawn, rather near the house, and the aspect would be very bleak without it. It is one of the tragedies of a new garden that all the trees must necessarily be very small, and I think we were extremely lucky to find one ready grown for us.

It took us several weeks to make our lawn. Making a lawn isn't just a matter of raking the surface and sowing grass seed. Certainly it wasn't for us. First of all the ground was by no means level and had to be levelled by driving in pegs at intervals. A long strip of wood with a spirit level strapped to it is placed on top of the pegs to get the right level.

We made all the mistakes imaginable because we were in such a hurry to get the job done. Our worst mistake was not to put in drainage. In light sandy or gravel soils this is not necessary but heavy clay like ours needs draining. A simple way of doing it is to dig a diagonal trench across the lawn, with a slight drop of an inch in a yard, to a corner where a pit is made filled with clinker (our brickbats could have been used). Agricultural pipes are put in the trench, covered with clinker, then gravel and lastly with earth. Tributary drains run into the main drain on each side, filled with clinker, gravel and earth. I have often considered draining our lawn but there never seems to be an opportunity for such a big operation, and we continue to have soggy patches where moss grows luxuriantly.

Another mistake we made was not to remove all the top soil before we started levelling. Walter thought it was sufficient to put some good sifted soil on top of the levelled ground, but I am sure one reason why we have such a poor lawn is because a lot of the infertile subsoil came to the top during the levelling process, and the precious bacteria and humus-laden top soil got buried underneath. I admit we grow excellent daisies and plaintain in our lawn but I am sure there is not sufficient depth of good soil under it to produce grass of velvety texture that is the hall-mark of a good lawn.

Sowing should be done in April or September. We chose September, and late September at that, but we should have done better to allow the soil to settle until the spring. We had to wait several days before the weather was right. It is no good sowing grass seed in a high wind, nor after heavy rain. The ideal moment is when the ground is not too dry and when a soft gentle rain is going to start after the sowing is done!

The levelled top soil should really be allowed to settle before it is raked to a fine tilth. Next the surface has to be firmed. We used a light roller, and this is quite satisfactory if the soil is not wet enough to stick to it. I have heard of people putting a sack of sand on a flat board and dragging that over the surface, and I believe in the old days gardeners had large flat wooden boards which they fastened to their feet with leather straps, rather like snow shoes.

It is most important to sow the seed evenly, and for this a double sowing is best. The lawn is divided by lines into sections a yard square. An ounce of grass seed is allowed for each square yard, and the first sowing is done walking up and down the lawn. Then the process is repeated walking across the lawn. We found the easiest way to get the right amount of seed was to measure it and for this we found a wineglass that just held an ounce.

After the seed is sown it must be raked well so that it is covered with earth, and then the surface has to be firmed again. After that we require gentle rain but, if it is not forthcoming, artificial watering must take its place, using a spray or a fine rose. The idea is to have the seed as closely embraced by damp earth as possible so that when germination takes place there are no air pockets to discourage the tiny thrusting roots. Birds sometimes enjoy a meal of grass seed, so it is really safest to cotton the ground after sowing.

Once a lawn is made it really should not require a lot of attention if it is cut regularly. To keep it in good condition a light dressing of granulated peat mixed with a little bonemeal and dried blood should be given in the winter. If there are weeds a selective weed-killer is used at the end of March, and in April a dressing of lawn sand will encourage new growth. Moss can be removed by raking and if rolling is done a spiked roller should be used to aerate the soil. Rolling with an ordinary roller does more harm than good, particularly with very heavy soils. The use of a lawn mower regularly gives it all the rolling it needs.

The question of dealing with the edge of a lawn is always a problem. If a paved path borders it there is no trouble, provided the path is slightly lower than the lawn so that the mower will not touch it when cutting the edge of the grass. But if a gravel path is next to the lawn there is always difficulty. The earth from the lawn inevitably falls on the gravel path, however carefully it is trimmed, and inevitably there is a crop of weeds at the edge of the path.

In the grand old gardens, which were made when cost did not matter, very often a neat stone coping was let into the ground, with a little gully between it and the lawn so that the mower could be used right up to the edge of the lawn. The gardens at Montacute House have neat rounded curbs of the local hamstone between all the lawns and paths. Very neat edgings can be made of concrete – not so awful as they sound because the concrete can be tinted to match the prevailing colour of the local stone, and then if they are still too new and glaring application of manure water will give them a weathered look.

We used stones between our lawn and the drive, but not even formal stones. Having enormous piles of rough hamstone from the various walls we had taken down, we thought it would be a good idea to build a low wall between the lawn and what was to be the drive. Our stones were all shapes and sizes but we chose the biggest and flattest and arranged them on top of each other, with earth between, to make a wall about eighteen inches high.

This was my first attempt at dry-stone-walling and I found it so fascinating that I repeated it in other parts of the garden. Between the stones and in every available crevice I tucked alpine plants. To begin with I hadn't very much beside white arabis and stonecrops, with some rock campanula, but now the little wall is much more interesting, with great mounds of lemon alyssum and rock roses, lavenders and helichrysums, erigerons and cheiranthus, and occasional groups of dwarf iris and *Campanula carpatica* on lower levels. Walter was very pleased with our first wall and egged me on to make others, but he was less enthusiastic as time went on as he thought I was spending too much time 'poking belly-crawlers into rat-holes' instead of doing jobs he thought more important.

I made quite a deep gully between the lawn and the little wall, to give room for the mower, and that I endeavour to keep weeded, the grass cut regularly and the edges nicely trimmed.

I cannot stress too much the importance of well-cut grass, good paths and well-trimmed hedges. With wifely stubbornness I am afraid I used to argue the point in my husband's lifetime, resenting his oft repeated assertion that my part of the garden – the flowers – didn't really matter. I know now that he was right when he said that the four essentials of a good garden are perfect lawns, paths, hedges and walls. No matter how beautiful they are, if the surroundings are unkempt, the flowers would give no pleasure, whereas one could have a perfectly good and satisfying garden without any flowers at all. I used to argue this point most heatedly but I have come to agree with him wholeheartedly. We all know how restful and beautiful a purely formal garden of grass and shaped trees can be. Italian gardens are lovely, and some of the formal gardens surrounding our stately homes would be spoilt by the introduction of flower beds. And we all know the feeling of dissatisfaction of seeing a garden full of the most wonderful plants, everything rare and exotic, but quite ruined by weeds, unkempt lawns and untidy paths. Walter would no more have left his grass uncut or the edges untrimmed than he would have neglected to shave. Do not think that he did not like flowers. He did very much, if they were properly grown and the setting was good. But he always looked at a garden as a whole, and the perfection of one plant did not compensate for neglect elsewhere.

# Making Paths

When it came to the job of making paths I discovered that this was a subject on which Walter had very strong views, and I had many lectures on how to achieve perfection. He felt that there was nothing to beat a good gravel path, and a good gravel path was so hard that nothing would spoil the surface and weeds would find no foothold.

Turning the barton into a well-made drive, big enough to take a dozen cars, was a big operation. We were lucky in being spared the problem of drainage. There is a big slope from the malthouse to the gate – as friends have discovered when they have not braked their cars properly!

The first thing we had to do was to level the surface, and then dig out the foundation. A good foundation is the secret of a good drive, we had it and there has never been any trouble since. I often wish we had taken as much trouble with our lawn as we did with the drive.

We had to dig out to a depth of nine and a half inches. Some of the stuff we removed could be used again, but it had to be sieved and the soil carted off to another part of the garden. The first layer was five inches of broken bricks and rubble – of which we had any amount. The garden boy rolled, Walter rammed and I sprinkled with the watering can. We rolled and rammed, rammed and rolled until the surface was as firm and level as a billiard table. The greatest care had to be taken at the edges of the drive, for that is where there is least traffic, and if there is any excuse at all the weeds grow there first.

The next layer was of finer stuff, ashes and clinker, to a depth of three inches. Again we rolled and watered over and over again until it was smooth and firm. There is no short cut to these operations but the heavier the roller used the quicker will perfection be reached.

Not less than an inch and a half of gravel had to be used for the top layer, and the laying of this was the longest operation of all, but the time and trouble we took paid us amply in the end.

First of all Walter had heaps of gravel dumped at regular intervals on the drive and then team work began. Walter spread the gravel, I watered it well and then the garden boy rolled. Each foot of drive was rolled and rolled and rolled, with a sprinkling of water between each rolling. Walter's theory was that the more you rolled the harder the surface, and the harder the surface the fewer the weeds. We took particular trouble again at the edges, for it is here that gravel is often loose and you really can't blame weeds for growing there.

It is quite important to see that the colour of the gravel goes well with your house and surroundings. Some gravel is really violent in colour and shrieks at everything in sight. But with a little trouble it is quite easy to find gravel or chippings that will harmonize with the garden scheme. When we first contemplated our drive we called on the local builder and asked if it would be possible to get fine hamstone chippings to harmonize with our hamstone house. That was not practicable but we were put on the track of some gravel that went with our house beautifully.

Every time we had heavy rain the drive and paths had to be rolled. It is very difficult to make the average garden help see the necessity for this, particularly in our rural corner where gardening from the village point of view is mostly vegetable growing, and paths and lawns quite a new idea. We had one boy who really enjoyed rolling the drive. He said it was a job after his own heart as he didn't have to think, and being very strong it was no effort to him to pull the heavy roller. He rolled very slowly too, which is the secret of good rolling. We lost him, alas, early in the war and never again did we have a good drive. Rolling was a job everyone shunned, and if it was done at all the roller was dragged round at a great rate, infinite care being taken to keep it away from the edges.

Even with constant rolling some weeds will appear and have to be exterminated, so about twice a year the whole surface was treated with weed-killer. We used either a solution of sodium chlorate or an arsenical weed-killer (we have no animals). Sodium chlorate acts on the leaves so a dry day is best for its application, but arsenical weed-killers have to percolate to the roots and one has to be very clever in choosing the right moment when the drive is receptively wet and when there is no danger of further rain to dilute the brew.

Walter always did the mixing and superintended the operation while the boy of the moment wielded the cans. It always seemed to me that they waited for a windy day for this job, and I had many anxious moments as wisps of poison spray were blown on my precious plants growing in the walls on each side of the path. In the end I took over the job myself and picked my own day.

My quarrel with gravel paths is that they require far more attention than most of us can possibly give under present day conditions. To keep them hard they must be rolled thoroughly very regularly, and once having achieved a modicum of perfection the proud owner is on constant tenterhooks that something will happen to spoil them. Walter used to get very worried if visitors drove the wrong way round our drive. One side was steep and it needed quite a lot of acceleration to get up and round the grass knoll in the middle of the drive. Every time we had a party there was an inquest the next morning and the roller had to come into action. Another source of annoyance was the dropping of earth on the drive. I always hoped Walter would not be present when I was swopping plants with my friends as most of them were quite oblivious that they were scattering earth all over the sacred drive. Vainly would I proffer the plants in a basket and hold it so close that no crumb should fall, but it never worked and there was always a nasty mess on the gravel and black looks for me.

After Walter's death I gave up the unequal struggle. It was impossible to keep the drive properly, and all the gravel was good for, from my point of view, was a convenient rooting medium for stray seeds. I could always count on a harvest of choice little seedlings in the drive. I thought I should lose this rich source of new plants when I had the main drive treated with a bituminous product and the other paths paved. But though I don't find so many now I still come across quite a few. Small rock plants still seed themselves on the hard surface of chippings rolled tight into this tar substance, and it makes me wonder if one might not get better results if a really hard surface was made on which to plant seeds. They may respond better to a little resistance. Various thymes come up near my little wall, rock statice and *Silene Schafta*\* in another place, and a gold mine of tiny primula seedlings near the narrow beds under the north walls where I grow candelabra primulas. There are far more primula seedlings in the path than in the beds – a most provoking habit of theirs, as it is difficult to prise them from the iron-hard surface without damaging their roots.

A good many people in our part of the world have solved the drive problem by covering the surface with loose chippings, either limestone or coarse gravel. This type of path does not appeal to me because I have never enjoyed walking on shingly beaches, and I don't think they are particularly labour-saving either. They have to be raked regularly to keep an even appearance and weeds grow very happily under the chippings and have to be poisoned from time to time, or hoed. Concrete is probably the only thing that can be relied upon to require no attention whatsoever, but the surface would have to have embedded in it either gravel or chippings to make it bearable, otherwise it would be impossibly glaring and soulless.

We used paving at the back of the house, and for the little path that led up to the barton. A paved path needs careful laying if it is to last. In our heavy clay we had to make a foundation of broken bricks, but on gravel or sandy soil this wouldn't be necessary. After ramming them down until the surface is quite level the stones are laid out, keeping the large ones with straight edges for the sides of the path, and smaller uneven ones to fill in between. To keep the stones firm and keep them from rocking they should be put down on joggles of cement, three or four to each stone. If nothing is to be allowed to grow between the stones the cracks are grouted with cement. It makes a vast amount of difference to the appearance if the grouting is left until the cement is nearly set then a small amount scooped out so that the outline of each stone is clearly defined. Walter used to stand over the men laying the paving and see that they did this. Most of them, if left to themselves, love to smear on the cement with a lavish hand so that parts of the stones are covered too.

I should have preferred to fill our cracks with a mixture of sand and fine soil so that tiny green plants would creep along all the stones but this was one thing Walter would not have at any price. I was allowed a very few very small holes, in which I planted thymes and Dresden China daisies, and the effect was far too neat and tidy. Time has improved things and a lot of the Somerset cement has become loosened, some of it helped, I admit, by a crowbar, and now I have little plants creeping and crawling in and out of nearly every crevice. The theory is that only my plants and not weeds grow in the cracks but a few weeds do appear, but they don't make as much work as Walter always prophesied they would.

# Clothing the Walls

We were surrounded by high walls and nothing was growing on any of them. The three-storey malthouse and the cowhouse, being strictly utilitarian, were starkly bare, nothing grew on the high wall along the road except tufts of arabis and an odd wallflower or two, and Walter was very anxious to clothe the end of the house where the old stones were too decayed to be repaired and the surface had been covered with stucco.

He sent me to the local nursery for ampelopsis by the dozen, we bought roses, pyracantha, cotoneaster and clematis. My sister gave us a *Ceanothus Veitchianus*\* for the front of the house, which was a sheet of blue in a very few years.

On the subject of clematis Walter was convinced that the ordinary blue *C. Jackmanii* was the only one worth growing. One day I was sent to the nursery for six of them. I had seen a red one I admired very much so I bought Walter his six blue ones and a Ville de Lyon for myself. When I got home there was much head shaking, and I was warned I was wasting my time and I should never get the results from my child that he would get from his little family.

I decided that my clematis should go on the wall near the gate, so I planted it with great care on the top terrace of the rock garden. Dainty little morsels of limy rubble were incorporated in the soil, a small bush of lavender was planted in front of it to keep the sun from its brittle stem, and I never allowed it to get dry. But in spite of all my cosseting it did not have a very robust childhood and it was some time before it began to enjoy life. Of course Walter's *Jackmaniis* went ahead without a hitch, just as he said they would, and the one on the south front of the house was really spectacular. People I met used to ask me if ours was the house with the wonderful blue clematis over the front door. In the end I did get two Ville de Lyon clematises to grow very well, and in time they were referred to as 'our red clematises' instead of a rather snooty 'your poor clematis'.

Walter took infinite trouble in training his clematises. Every day he would indicate to each leaf over which wire it should go and he got obedience. Under his management each trail was separate and each clematis covered vast surfaces of wall, with each bloom getting its full value. When I saw Walter standing on the rock garden coaxing my Ville de Lyon to spread her wings I said nothing but I recognized it as a major triumph.

Now that I have to train these beautiful but temperamental plants myself I marvel at his patience and the wonderful results he got. I induce the trails to start on their journey away from the parent stem but directly my back is turned they slide off my wires and lock themselves in a firm embrace with their brothers and sisters. It is well-nigh impossible to disentangle them from this huddle and start them off again on their outward trek. The stems are brittle and break with the slightest excuse. And even if I do separate one stem from the family the next morning I usually find it has ceased adventuring to the unknown and is again hugging itself. The consequence is that instead of large spaces covered with well-trained flowers I get a great lump of leaves and flowers which is too heavy for its frail twining contact with the supporting wires, and gets blown all over the place by the wind.

Wire netting stretched up the wall on which clematises grow is a good way of teaching them to spread themselves and far better than the cat's cradle of wires which I use. And while we are talking of clematises I'd like to mention how lovely they look growing over a lowish wall, rather like a beautiful oriental carpet flung over the wall, and here wire netting is essential to indicate to them just how much of the wall you want them to cover. With wire netting they cling quite naturally, but with wires it helps to attach the tendrils where you think they should go with little strips of wired green paper (like the stiffeners the laundry use in collars) sold by garden shops.

The roses on the front of the house grew luxuriantly and Walter trained them close to the windows so that we caught glimpses of Mme Abel Chatenay and Lady Hillingdon peeping in at us while we had our meals.

One of the things we admired most when we were house-hunting in the district was the effect of red roses on the mellow hamstone walls. So we had quite a number of Paul's Scarlet* and Climbing General McArthur on the front and sides of the house. The new polyantha Frensham is wonderfully effective as a bush grouped against a background of hamstone walls, and blooms over a very long period.

Walter realized that it would be some time before the climbers would make an effect on the bare walls, so one day, without telling me, he bought a collection of stuffed heads and mounted horns at a London sale room. Very soon heads, antlers and horns sprouted from every available wall, inside and out. The malthouse received the most imposing pieces from the collection, and very soon our house wasn't known as 'the one with the lovely blue clematis on the front' but as 'the house with all the heads on the outbuildings'. In a community largely composed of retired army people this display was definitely surprising, if not a little shocking. One adorned one's house with one's own trophies but it was rather unusual to buy them by the gross. Walter used to chuckle about his heads and was delighted when he could tell an enquirer that he had bought them and not shot them himself!

Luckily the ones outside didn't last long. Not being intended to withstand rain and snow the skin soon came apart and flapped open before falling in the drive, the fillings disintegrated, the painted mouths and red nostrils were washed away and before long all that was left were the horns starkly mounted on a narrow length of wood. When they got to this stage I was allowed to put them on the bonfire, but I am still occasionally reminded of them when I am digging and see a large liquid brown eye gazing up at me.

Since Walter died I have cut down the ampelopsis because during these fifteen years they have grown so vigorously that they were trying to push off the roof, and attaching themselves to all the windows. To fill the gaps a passion flower now wreathes the rain water barrel by the malthouse, a *Forsythia suspensa* is working its way up another wall. Walter could never be persuaded to have a wisteria because he said they would take too long to flower. Now I have two, and both flowered about two years after I planted them. Another climber I always hankered for was a bignonia, and in this case Walter was quite right not to indulge me. I put one in myself, it grew so robustly that I could not curb it, I was always hacking at it to enable me to see out of my bedroom windows, but it never flowered, so it had to go. But it has not gone yet, it keeps reappearing quite unabashed, and I keep digging it out. I put in a *Chimonanthus fragrans** in place of the bignonia and it is more rewarding. It flowered – just – after about two years, and every year I get a few more of its heady-perfumed flowers. No garden is complete without this wonderful winter shrub, planted as near the house as possible so that one can enjoy its perfume without venturing far into the cold. *Chimonanthus fragrans lutea** is another exciting shrub. The blossom is all yellow, in a delicate shade, and to see its waxy flowers with the wintry sun shining through them makes one wonder if they are real. I believe this form is more difficult to propagate than the more usual variety, so it is rather expensive, but what a lovely way to be extravagant.

Another newcomer to the front of the house is a stauntonia. I hope it will prosper in this sheltered spot and I look forward to its scented green flowers. On the north wall facing the house I have put a *Garrya elliptica*, with its neat evergreen leaves and graceful swaying tassels of palest green arriving most happily in the winter. It is worth taking a magnifying glass to study the exquisite workmanship of these super catkins.

Against the pink brick wall at the end of the malthouse there is another winter-flowering shrub, *Lonicera fragrantissima*. The white waxy flowers of this honeysuckle are wonderfully fragrant, but for picking are rather swamped by the luxuriant green of the foliage. I find if I pick them they look far more attractive if the leaves are taken off the flowering stems, using some sprays of leaves that have no flowers, with them.

A plant I like and have in various parts of the garden is *Phygelius capensis*. This too is evergreen, with dark glossy leaves. It is often used as a bush and I don't think it makes a very satisfactory one as it grows unevenly and needs constant checking. But plant it against a sheltered wall and it will reach five or six feet. Its large sprays of tubular flowers, brick red in colour, are generously given and come in the late summer and autumn when there is too much lavender and yellow in the garden. If happy this plant is inclined to encroach on less assertive plants, and has to be curbed. Less invasive is its more refined brother *Phygelius aequalis*. It does not grow so quickly and its flowers are longer and paler, and delicately touched with green.

*Eucalyptus Gunnii* is growing well against the south wall of the cowhouse. This is the hardiest of all the eucalyptus family and has come through several hard winters very well. It needs tying back firmly, as I discovered when to my horror a gale snapped off the top. In brilliant sunshine the fluttering leaves make delicate shadow effects on the wall. Its grey-green foliage is delightful for decoration and lasts a very long time in water. When flowers are scarce early in the year I use the new leaf tips of clear pink instead of flowers in the house.

# Hedges

After clothing the walls, Walter turned his attention to hedges. We had our high wall on one side and we wanted something equally high and impenetrable on the other side and along a low wall beyond the house on the south side. Our thoughts turned to *Cupressus macrocarpa*. We were warned that it had a limited life, in fact, just when we were considering our hedge the local doctor showed us a magnificent hedge he had planted at the back of his tennis court the year his son was born. That year his son was thirteen and the hedge was beginning to die. Of course we did not heed and we planted macrocarpa along the road beyond the house and between ourselves and the next house. The hedge flourished. It was well clipped every August and gave us no trouble. But in 1951, thirteen years after it was planted I noticed several of the trees were dying. Our hedge hasn't made such a wholesale job of it as the doctor's did but I have two nasty gaps where four or five trees had to be dug out. Now I have started a new hedge of *Lonicera nitida* behind so that I shan't have to wait too long for a screen after the rest of the macrocarpa die.

I have heard many explanations for this behaviour of the macrocarpa. I used to think it had only a limited life because its roots found something they didn't like when they got down below a certain level. A nurseryman has at last solved the problem for me. It is the regular clipping that does it. Macrocarpa, unlike yew, needs to breathe through its trunk to survive. The tight clipping makes the foliage denser and cuts off all air from the centre of the tree. The correct way to deal with macrocarpa is to thin as well as trim. The trained gardener pecks out little tufts here and there with his sécateurs and lets in air. All shaped cupressus trees should be treated in the same way, and it is remarkable how they respond to such treatment.

The one thing I did directly we bought the house was to plant a hedge parallel with the back of the house to hide the back door and kitchen. My sister gave me enough little plants of *Lonicera nitida* to start us off and these I planted with the idea of screening entirely the back premises. It is difficult now to understand our point of view and remarkable that things could have changed so completely in such a short time. For in those days it was unthinkable that ladies and gentlemen enjoying themselves in the garden should be disturbed by the sight of tradesmen delivering food at the back door. We even put 'Tradesmen' on the back gate! And the lower half of the window at the pantry sink, which overlooked the garden, was discreetly glazed with ground glass. No one must see the maid washing up, but it never occurred to us, the architect or the builder how dull it was for the poor girl to be shut off like that. When the war came and I spent hours at the sink I adopted my sister's suggestion and had clear glass put in that window. I enjoyed the garden and planned my next job while I washed the breakfast things. I got a lot of good ideas too, even if I did finish the war with hardly one of our original cups or plates!

The little hedge had a difficult childhood. My sister had generously given us small cuttings that she had struck for herself and they were very tiny to face life with such hazards. Early in the spring the builders took possession and we could no longer live in the house. Pipes for central heating, boards, bricks and all the other things that go with building were heaped everywhere, and I shall never cease to marvel at the tenacity with which that little hedge stuck to life. My aristocratic gardening friends refer to it as 'the common hedge', but I know nothing else that would have survived and prospered. We used to drive down from London to see how the builders were getting on, and the first thing I did when we arrived on the scene was to walk over to my hedge and remove the worst of the debris. Very soon the builders began to realize where my affections were centred and as soon as we drove in at the gate there would be a scurry to free the hedge from its encumbrance of building material.

With cuttings from that little hedge I made all our other hedges. To break the garden we planted small hedges in various places. One went across the top garden between the flowers and a small orchard, another at right angles to screen the small vegetable garden, and two rectangular enclosures were hedged at the back of the malthouse to hide heaps of compost, manure, peat and leaf mould.

The garden high-brows may sneer at 'the common hedge' but it really is the easiest and most accommodating hedge material I know. Whenever we decided we'd like a hedge all I had to do was to prepare the ground, put in a line (I tied knots in my line at nine-inch intervals for sowing broad beans and planting hedges) and then stick in my cuttings. It doesn't seem to matter at what time of the year one takes cuttings but they should be of hard wood. I generally use cuttings of about nine inches in length, as straight as possible and after taking off all the side branches from the bottom half push that part into the soil.

The most important thing when taking cuttings is to see that the earth is pressed as firmly as possible against the cutting, particularly the base from which the tiny roots will soon appear. If they find kind mother earth ready to receive them these little roots take heart and venture further, but if they meet a vacuum they become discouraged. In heavy, lumpy soil it is always safer to use sand or sand and peat. Such a mixture makes an inviting reception for the infant roots, but it must be pressed as tightly as possible to the cutting, starting at the bottom. Some people use a small dibber for this but I feel safer with my fingers, as I know what I am doing. For a screening hedge, such as that used round a compost heap, I put in the cuttings in a single row, nine inches apart, but for a wider, more important hedge, say in front of a garden, a double row, staggered, with a foot between each cutting, is better. After watering I press down the earth on each side, then cut off the tops of the cuttings to encourage side growth.

I find that *Lonicera nitida* roots with the slightest excuse, in fact it can be a nuisance because if any little piece is left on the bed after trimming the hedge, it will root. I suffered badly from this until we started using a wide piece of hessian on each side of the hedge to catch all the trimmings.

We made a mistake with our first hedge in not cutting it down more drastically. We were so anxious for it to grow high enough to hide that disgraceful back door that it wasn't trimmed properly for a long time, merely cut level. The consequence is that it did not grow thick at the bottom. After twelve years it was nearly four feet wide at the top but only a foot in width at the roots. Though we kept it well clipped the nature of the plant is not equal to the strain of supporting so much flesh. It waved about in the wind, quivering like a jelly, and when there was no wind the line was floppy and undulating. To bring it back it had to be cut down to two feet in height, and cut back so that the top is slightly narrower than the base, and it will continue to be trimmed in this tapering fashion. The cutting back process is not pretty. For several months there were only bare branches to be seen, with horrid maimed stumps, and I received many condolences on the death of my hedge. I explained I had done it myself and I was certain the disfigurement was only temporary. It was during the winter that we dealt so drastically with it, and sure enough in the spring tiny leaves began to appear on those bare branches, and very soon it was as green as ever and needed clipping again. None of the other hedges were as bad as this one, as they were trimmed earlier in their youth, but all have a tendency to get too wide at the top and now we are very firm with them.

Heavy snow is liable to make temporary havoc of *Lonicera nitida* and some people cut their hedges like a roof instead of flat to avoid this trouble.

One has always to take the rough with the smooth, and the advantage of a quick-growing hedge means the disadvantage of constant clipping. Four times a year is the minimum required and in between it may need a slight hair cut if one wants to be particularly trim for a particular occasion. If one has only a small hedge a good way of keeping it in check is to cover the sides and top with wire netting and trim down to that. It wouldn't be possible to use an electric trimmer on a hedge so treated and therefore it is only practicable on a scale that can be covered by hand clipping. An electric hedge clipper is a great boon for hedges such as mine and I don't know what we should do without it. It makes a better job of the trimming with straighter lines and more clean-cut edges.

*Lonicera nitida* is the most obliging hedge material. It doesn't mind being shaped like yew, and I have seen extremely good birds and animals cut from it. It makes a very good little edging hedge instead of box, and can be kept just as small as a box hedge. Some of the cottages in this village have trained it into green porches by dint of careful and regular trimming, and I know one house where it has been grown as a great solid block of close green over six feet high for a screen. In fact you can use it in any way you want but you must go on trimming it regularly.

A lavender hedge can be grown just as easily, although not so quickly as a lonicera one. Cuttings pushed into the soil root very easily. When making either a lonicera or lavender hedge it is a good plan to have a little cache of spare plants in an odd corner. Some of the hedge cuttings may be obstinate and refuse to root and then you have a reserve of the same sized plants to fill in the gaps. Santolina makes a delightful silver hedge and can be clipped like lavender.

Some gardens call for a natural hedge and here there is wonderful scope. Hardy fuchsias look lovely falling over a wall, *Kerria japonica* rewards one with its bright golden flowers, and for a taller hedge there are laurustinus, old-fashioned roses or cypresses. In a very big garden tall cypress trees, grown without clipping, make a delightful background and save a great deal of work.

I persuaded Walter to put a beech hedge round the orchard. It took a lot of persuasion because for years he had complained that beeches were still clothed in their brown winter leaves when all the rest of the trees were gaily flaunting their delicate spring green. He agreed to beech in the end because we didn't want quickthorn, the price of yew would have been prohibitive and we didn't think anything else would be at all suitable for an orchard. In the end Walter became quite attached to his cosy brown hedge. Though he didn't mind it in the winter he complained in the spring, but agreed that the delicate green of the leaves when they did come was worth waiting for. One clipping a year in August is all it requires and I still think that decision was a good one. Perhaps we might have made it copper beech but that, I think, is a little too refined for an orchard. In a garden copper beech is lovely and I often wonder why more people do not put in hedges of this in their gardens. I know several and they are always a delight to me.

# The Terraced Garden

While the lawn and drive were being made I had to work as a labourer with Walter and the garden boy, but when they were finished I was at last permitted to go off and amuse myself in what was to be my part of the garden, the flower beds. I had long been considering what should be done with the ground on the west of the house. This was on a higher level than the rest and sloped up to a small orchard. We were lucky that our garden was on different levels. A garden that is completely flat is difficult to make interesting. We all know gardens that start as a field and finish as a field, no matter what the owners do in the way of trouble and expense. The kindest thing fate can do to you is to give you a garden that slopes away from the house. The upward slope is more difficult to deal with as great care has to be taken that it does not become top heavy.

When we bought the house this part of the garden rose sharply to the orchard without path or form. The speculator who sold the house to us had put in a few miserable gooseberry bushes, but they were choked with couch grass. In fact, it was nothing but a wilderness and looked the most uninspiring material for a garden.

Walter had no particular views about what should be done here. He agreed that I could have it for flowers and left it at that. The work of the garden had divided itself unconsciously. Walter took over the care of the grass, paths, walls and hedges and left the flowers (and most of his clearing up) to me.

It was getting towards winter when I started. I studied the ground for days on end, looked at it from every angle, drew plans on paper and, by degrees, ideas took shape.

The first thing to do was to make a path up to the orchard, and this I decided must be slightly curving. The lay-out was irregular so we couldn't have anything too formal, and my idea was to have something simple and cottagey to go with the long low house.

To get the first level I made low, stone steps, with a fairly high wall to support the earth. On this level I made very wide paths to give the feeling of space. They were gravelled in Walter's day but since then I have paved them, and now the effect is of a gracious terrace.

I decided to make the garden on each side of the path a series of terraces, each terrace supported by a low wall, in which I planned to grow rock plants. Paths were to be made between the terraces.

I didn't realize at the time that I was setting myself the hardest task any gardener could have. Everyone knows that the easiest border to arrange is one against a wall or hedge. A double border which must be attractive from both sides is difficult, but what I was trying to do was to make a series of borders, each of which must look well from four angles and must also combine with the borders in front and behind. I had three terraces on the left, and three on the right, but on this side I had to dovetail in a fourth, triangular bed to fill up the space.

We all know the saying about fools. When I think of it now I wonder how I had the hardihood to attempt such an ambitious scheme. I had never done any gardening before we went to Somerset and had certainly never even thought about garden design. It might have been the most abysmal failure, but I didn't think about that. My only thought was to get the project under way before Walter took an interest in what I was doing and complicated matters with too much criticism and advice.

We had a very early fall of snow that year and I can remember walking out my plan in the snow. Walter was a fair-weather gardener and I knew he'd busy himself with indoor jobs while the weather was bad and leave me to my own devices.

First of all I dug out trenches and made my low dry stone walls in them. We had a liberal supply of stones and I was able to choose fairly even pieces and made quite presentable little walls.

After the walls were done I dug out the earth in front of them to make paths between the terraced beds. It was then that Walter made an appearance and was quite horrified at what he saw. 'Why on earth are you making canyons?' I explained that they were the paths and begged him to be patient. The weather was still bad and he was full of indoor schemes so he left me to the mud and chaos.

Levelling the beds was the worst job of all. I knew enough to save the top soil and take away the clay underneath, but the problem was what to do with the stuff. I had heaps of good soil all over the place where I was working and the clay had to be wheeled right away and dumped somewhere in the lower garden. The only way to get it there was down a plank over the stone steps. It was cold and damp with mud everywhere and the wheelbarrow was always tipping itself over as my unskilful hands tried to balance it on the greasy plank.

Luckily it was a mild, if wet winter, and by the early spring I had done most of the work. It didn't meet with approval and I admit it did look bleak. Every morning at breakfast I was greeted with 'Stones, stones, stones!' Or it might be a query: 'How is the floral quarry this morning?' Walter's bathroom overlooked that part of the garden and as he liked to dawdle over his bath and shaving he had ample opportunity to gaze with horror on what I had done the day before.

He evidently thought about it for when the day came when I had finished the construction work and was ready to start planting he said 'Now we'll put in the pole roses.' 'The what?' I asked, aghast. As the house was a low one, and was built on a very much lower level than this part of the garden, I had planned to plant my beds with low-growing plants, to give a tapestry effect, and if I wanted any very tall things they were to go at the back and at the sides. I had widened the path winding up between the beds and it was on either side of this path that the roses, trained up their poles, were to be planted. And they were. There was nothing I could do to stop it, no argument had any effect. Walter assured me that they would be the making of my garden and I'd like them in the end, so they were planted with due care and ceremony and I had to plan my planting round them.

I can't remember all the roses we chose; there was nothing very outstanding among them except, perhaps, Cupid, which I think is one of the loveliest of climbers, with its large single shell-pink flowers and golden stamens. It has the most devastating thorns I know but I can even forgive it that lustiness for the beauty of its flowers. Others we chose were Chaplin's Pink, Climbing Lady Hillingdon and General McArthur, Melody, Paul's Scarlet* and some very old ones such as Gloire de Dijon and Wm Allen Richardson.

I discovered that it was unwise for me to plant too near the roses. This was not only because their wandering branches clawed my hair and scratched my hands, but to keep out of the way of the manure with which Walter fed them. Walter believed in manuring with a very generous hand and woe betide any little plant of mine that grew nearby, as it would surely die of suffocation under the great gollops of manure that were plastered round every rose. All the manure we could get was devoted to the roses and dahlias. Neither of us was very concerned about the welfare of the vegetables. If sometimes I thought any of my children were in need of a little stimulant I had to steal little bits from the roses when my husband was not looking. When I was doing this I always remembered his oft repeated belief that women had no sense of honesty!

When, later on, we were able to get more manure and I was allowed a little Walter did not like the way I used it. He always accused me of being mean with manure, and disliked very much the way I used it on my flower beds. I was so frightened of getting the manure on the plants that I took endless care to dot the ground with small pieces, well away from the plants. As we drove round the countryside Walter delighted in pointing out the massive heaps of manure dumped quite close together all over the fields, waiting to be spread. 'That is the way to use manure,' he'd say, 'not the way you put it on.' I still use manure sparingly on the flower beds. We spread it lavishly in the kitchen garden but only the roses, and such things as delphiniums, phlox and dahlias, which have very big appetites, get really big helpings. Christmas roses like some manure in the summer; it helps to keep them moist if it is not possible to give them plenty of water. Many people consider too much manure on the flower garden produces too luxuriant foliage at the expense of the flowers. It depends, I think, on your soil and what you take out of it. I cram my beds with plants and feed them well, and my hard clay soil needs plenty of humus. Even if you are not a manure fan it is not a bad idea to water your plants with manure flavoured water just before they are coming into bloom. If you have no liquid manure, to be well diluted before being used, it is quite easy to drop a small sack of manure into a watering can, leave it for a while and use the infusion. The plants will show their gratitude by giving even better blooms than they did before.

# Planting

I learnt a great deal from Walter that first year of gardening. The first thing I learnt was that he knew a great deal more about the subject than I thought he did. I was a complete novice, and I thought that he was too. I knew he had had gardens and gardeners, but I assumed that being very busy he had left all the planning and work to them. I may say I got very tired of one particular gardener during that first year. He was quoted at me morning, noon and night until I came to hate his name. Everything he did was perfect, he never neglected anything and he always did all the jobs that needed doing at the right time. It was no good for me to tell Walter that I had to sandwich my gardening between housekeeping, household jobs and a certain amount of social life. In his opinion there was no excuse for not getting things done at the right time.

Another of his gardeners had my sympathy, and I think there was a moral for me in the tale of his undoing. This man had one joy in life and that was to grow wonderful chrysanthemums in pots to bring into the house in the winter. According to Walter he used to stroke and fondle his chrysanthemums so much that he was neglecting the rest of the garden. Remonstrances had no effect so one day Walter took a knife and slashed off all those pampered darlings at ground level. It was by remembering this episode that I learnt to have a sense of proportion and fairness in my gardening, and not devote too much time to the things I like best at the expense of the rest of the garden.

The first inkling I had that Walter held very definite views was concerning the level of the flower beds. I had always seen them raised above the surrounding grass or path, and I made mine in the same way. I suppose the original idea was for better drainage and to allow one to get the best possible view of the plants. Rose gardens are still often made in this way, and one sees it in parks and public gardens. I never thought of it before Walter pointed it out, but the whole idea is superficial and a bed that is absolutely flush with the path or lawn looks larger and far more attractive. Now that I have paved paths I am even more enthusiastic over the idea as I plant sprawlers as near the path as possible so that they spill over the path and break the hard line. In Walter's day I had to be careful that nothing spilled over the path, which was then gravelled, as the roller did not recognize the rights of sprawlers. A plant that benefits from this level of planting is *Gentiana acaulis*. It likes being trodden on and I plant borders of it so close to the path that they regularly receive attention from my full-sized feet.

We used some of our plentiful supply of stones to keep the beds separate from the gravel paths. In my ignorance I first put them in vertically so that several inches protruded above the ground, but after it was pointed out to me I realized that the effect was far pleasanter and just as effective if they were laid flat. One thing Walter taught me was to avoid unnecessary distractions. One must have something to separate flower beds from paths but one should not draw attention to the border and so detract from the flowers themselves.

It is surprising that in quite good gardens one often sees a gravel path merging straight into a flower bed. It is bad for the path because earth inevitably mixes with the gravel and one gets more weeds than ever. Something neat is needed, that blends into a picture. We were lucky in having plenty of stones, and I was able to pick out flat, even-shaped stones with one straight edge at least. These were laid very carefully so that they were level on top and the straight sides were used to make the edge of the path. If I'd had straight paths I should have used a line, but I had to rely on my eye to get a straight effect for my curving paths. Some people use bricks, and they look quite well if laid flat, particularly if there are brick paths. Sometimes they are put in diagonally to make a jagged edge, and that I think is a pity, rather reminiscent of the horrid little fancy tiles so beloved by Victorian gardeners. I'd treat them both the same way and cover them up at once with luxuriant greenery if I couldn't remove them altogether. Sometimes one sees shells in cottage gardens, which may be quaint but are neither very effective or attractive. Unobtrusive concrete mouldings are as good as anything if they are laid almost on the level of the path and are weathered to match the gravel.

In some gardens plants make a successful edging. In the more spacious days little box hedges were the answer, but cost and labour these days make them a luxury. London Pride or thrift can both be grown in an even band and need little attention. A low lavender hedge is sometimes used, and in wide borders, where something massive is in keeping, megasea or *Stachys lanata*\* are ideal, or even acanthus where space is really no object. Some of the tight growing mossy saxifrages will keep the peace between path and bed, or even those sturdy double daisies that grow about four inches high. I have seen nepeta clipped as a hedge but that is a sacrilege. The whole beauty of nepeta is its graceful loose way of life, and soft blue flowers, and to confine it to rectangular form is most unappreciative. With paved paths there is no problem. The earth comes right up to the path and gives several inches of extra space in which to plant.

On the whole I had very little interference with the way I planted my beds, but I was urged to prevent monotony by having an occasional tall plant right in the front of the beds. I obeyed this so literally with some lupins that one had in the end to be sacrificed because it got so enormous, so I chose my accents more carefully afterwards. It was Walter who gave me the idea of planting groups of irises right at the edge of the path, so that their clean upward thrust made contrast with the low-growing plants on either side. He also taught me the value of massed effects, so instead of an odd delphinium dotted here and there, as I would have planted them, he insisted that they were planted in groups of five or six. I realized that this was the only way to avoid a spotty effect.

I went through some dreadful times when I first started planting. In spite of all my efforts quite a lot of clay was left in the soil, and the harsh March winds whipped it into hard nodules which made the most uncomfortable homes for my newly planted creatures. I know better now and, though I have improved the soil immeasurably, I always use a mixture of sand and peat when planting, particularly with small things. Then I see that the roots are spread out and every little fibre has close contact with this good rooting material. Such treatment makes them feel snug and at home and they hardly know they have been unrooted from one place and transported to another. The worst thing you can do to a plant is to permit an air pocket anywhere near its roots, and this is what I am ashamed to say I did when I first began gardening. My planting was so insecure that the plants lurched about in the bed and were blown this way and that by the wind. Like a woman holding on to her hat they were too busy trying to keep a foothold in the earth to give a thought to anything else. Firm planting is one of the first essentials, and it is a good idea to give a little tug to anything that is just put in to make sure it is firmly anchored. I always test my cuttings in the same way, though not quite so vigorously.

Firmness in all aspects is a most important quality when gardening, not only in planting but in pruning, dividing and tying up. Plants are like babies, they know when an amateur is handling them. My plants knew, but I didn't. Walter would not tolerate an unhealthy or badly grown plant and if he saw anything that wasn't looking happy he pulled it up. Often I would go out and find a row of sick-looking plants laid out like a lot of dead rats. It became something like a game. If I knew I had an ailing child I was trying to bring round I'd do my utmost to steer him away from that spot. It didn't often work and now I realize that he was right in his contention that a plant that had begun to grow badly could never be made into a decent citizen and the only thing to do was to scrap it. Sweet Williams were my greatest trial until I learned to cheat. Mine had an awful way of becoming leggy and untidy, and instead of sitting up straight and sturdily they flopped about and lolled about in a way most unpleasing to my lord and master. I should have saved myself a lot of anguish if I had discovered earlier that a lot can be done by putting the unseemly legginess under the soil, and making it so firm that each spike is supported. I have even used this unorthodox treatment for pinks that straggled, to make them temporarily presentable. Of course, the real answer is to grow and plant them properly.

Another thing I was taught was to get plants into the soil at the first possible moment. It really hurt my husband when people bought or were given plants and delayed planting them. Sometimes we'd see a border being remade and heaps of plants left lying about with their roots exposed to the air. It is so easy to cover the roots with sacks if one hasn't time to heel them in, and it makes all the difference to the life of the plant.

Planting came first in our lives and whatever job was on hand it had to be abandoned if plants arrived. I remember one weekend when we had some rather special visitors, to whom we were showing the countryside. A parcel of flowering shrubs was delivered by the railway. The visitors just had to amuse themselves while we dealt with those shrubs. First we put their roots in a bucket of water while we dug the holes, then Walter planted them feverishly and I watered them copiously while our visitors looked on and thought we were slightly mad.

Sometimes, with the best intentions in the world, it isn't possible to plant immediately, but one can always dig a hole and heel the plants in the earth, or with trees or shrubs that are too big to plant like that, one can see that the roots are covered with straw or sacking. I have given plants to people – and kind people at that – and seen those same plants weeks later huddled together in a corner just as I had taken them from my basket, without a crumb of soil or a handful of leaves. When I give away plants I like to pack them in damp moss so that they come to no harm if neglected. One can do that with a few small treasures but it takes too long when giving away large quantities, and the only thing to do is to choose the people to whom you give them.

One mistake nearly all beginners make is to plant too close together. I heard a lot about this when I first started gardening, jokes on the subject were read out to me, and I came to the conclusion that most humorists were male, because it was always the wife who made this silly mistake. It is extremely difficult to visualize how big your plants will grow, and it is quite natural to want to cover that expanse of bare earth as quickly as possible. In fact if you planted the things as far apart as they ought to be the effect would be very bare and bleak for a long time, but it is the only thing to do. Most people plant shrubs far too close together and the effect is completely ruined when they grow up. It is far, far better to plant them at the right distances and fill the gaps in the early stages with temporary plantings. It is sometimes worth while to put in more shrubs than you will eventually want if quick results are needed. I did this with *Euphorbia Wulfenii** in a place where I wanted a quick screen. Three plants were put in fairly close together and I had my effect in the first year. The strongest of the three overlaid the other two, and I removed them. The beginnings of a garden need not be painfully bare if you plant less worthy subjects among your permanent collection.

It requires great faith to allow the right amount of space when planting, but when you do the results are surprising. Michaelmas daisies, as an example, if grown properly with individual shoots about a foot apart (half the height is the usual allowance) make themselves into fat bushy plants which are a joy to behold (and need a stout stake to uphold). Annuals should be thinned out ruthlessly and instead of spindly specimens those that are left will show you what can be done when a plant has adequate space in which to develop. I have seen a single plant of night-scented stock make a bush about eighteen inches square, not because of my strongmindedness, I fear, but owing to the fact that all its little brothers and sisters died in infancy and it was left alone.

# Staking

When it came to staking I came to grief badly. In the first place I did not stake early enough, and quite a lot of handsome heads of flowers were condemned by my mentor because they were crooked by the time I did tie them up. Nothing will straighten a plant that has grown crooked. And when I did stake I was accused of doing it too loosely. My idea was to allow the plants to grow as naturally as I could so I put a few sticks at the outside of each clump and tied string – not too tightly – to the sticks. I admit it wasn't satisfactory because the wind blew the flowers about mercilessly in my little enclosures and they got tangled and bent. I was warned that I must be more drastic but took no heed. So Walter taught me a lesson. He got stout stakes (mine were slight because I didn't want them to show too much) and he drove them into the ground with a mallet. Then he took those poor unsuspecting flowers, put a rope round their necks and tied them so tightly to the stake that they looked throttled. He put into the action all the exasperation he felt at a pig-headed woman who just would not learn. I did learn then, because I knew what would happen to my poor flowers if my staking was sloppy. I never achieved the perfection that was preached to me, that is, a stick for each stem, but I was more generous with sticks and I made an elaborate cage of string between them so that the flowers had little play. Most people use twigs or peasticks for their staking and it is quite successful in ordinary soil, but I never succeeded because I couldn't get the rough sticks sufficiently deep into my heavy clay, and they were never firm. I could use a mallet with straight sticks, and though it made more work, it was the only thing to do.

There are, of course, other good ways of supporting one's flowers. In a very big border, full of big plants, coarse netting stretched over posts gives magnificent support. For individual plants there are excellent wire circles that are placed flat on the ground over the plant and raised on upright supports as it develops. With this method the plant starts right and gives no trouble at all, but it is not very easy to use these supports on very big clumps without a lot of wasteful overlapping.

Now I use metal supports in the form of a half circle with long prongs that are pushed into the ground. I copied the idea from a friend and got the local blacksmith to make them for me in all weights, sizes and heights. To preserve them and to make them less conspicuous I have painted them dark green. Sometimes I use two to make a complete circle, or one with string tied behind it. In large plantings half a dozen or more can be used at different angles and for supporting plants along a wall they are ideal, as the flowers hang over slightly in a natural way. I make a practice of putting them in very early, pushing them in a long way to begin with, and pulling them up as the stalks grow taller. When one lot of plants have finished blooming and no longer need support I lift out the wires and put them in to help the next lot of plants that are coming on.

There are people who will not admit the necessity for tying up their plants, and their gardens are always a depressing sight. There is only one way to avoid staking and that is to grow only plants that never need any artificial support – but what a lot of lovely things would be missed if one did that.

# Gardening with a Knife

Walter had one garden adage he was always quoting at me: 'It is nice to take a walk in the garden and better still if you take a hoe with you.' I think a pair of sécateurs would be my choice.

How often one sees odd bits of dead wood, suckers and overhanging branches as well as deadheads on one's morning amble. That timely snip saves a lot of time and trouble, and one can collect a few flowers for the house at the same time.

Deadheading is a most important part of gardening. It isn't only from the point of tidiness that one should remove spent flowers. A plant will go on flowering over much longer periods if every dead bloom is removed at once. Kept in a state of frustrated motherhood it will go on producing flowers in the hope of being allowed to set seed and thus reproduce itself. I often get three flowerings on Canterbury Bells by persistent deadheading, and I even deadhead my naturalized daffodils so that they do not deteriorate. I have some old swords and I keep one sharpened for this job. One can slash off a lot of heads in a very short time.

My friends are not so keen on this habit of mine, it deprives them of all the exciting seeds they would like. The only plants I allow to come to maturity are those which I want to increase, such as primulas and cyclamen, willow gentian, blue poppies and incarvillea.

Walter was never tired of telling me about a certain great garden, whose noble owner boasted that no dead flower would ever be found therein – a wonderful standard which we'd all like to copy. I often wondered how many gardeners were employed in that garden, and if there were many beds of violas in it.

We used to have great arguments about this deadheading job. Walter used to go round with a pair of sécateurs in his hand and snip off his dead roses, but he never picked them up. I complained that I wasn't the fifth gardener and it wasn't my job to go round clearing up after him. But I always did because I couldn't bear to see the beds littered with dead flowers. In the end it became a family joke and he took great delight in telling me when various parts of the garden needed the attentions of the fifth gardener. He pruned roses in the same way and, when I protested, always explained that the important thing was to get the pruning done and the little matter of collecting the prunings could be done at any time – but never by him!

I think a good many gardeners would have better gardens if they used sécateurs now. Most plants respond to quite severe cutting down. Aubrietia, for instance, should be cut right down to the ground the moment it shows signs of getting brown and leggy. It responds magnificently to this treatment and is very soon covered with a new crop of tight green leaves, and before you know where you are is flowering a second time. Some people take shears to their aubrietia but I think sécateurs make a better job as they cut closer.

Rock roses, too, should be cut back when they get straggly, dead parts of rock phlox should be cut out, and such things as saponaria and dianthus need drastic cutting. Yellow alyssum can be made to live up to its name 'compactum' if everything is cut away after flowering. One wouldn't think that the plant would be satisfied with a few stumps of stems, and looks maimed for life, but in a surprisingly short time it covers itself with neat young leaves. If it is not cut like this the stalks get long and top heavy and break off at the joint.

Nepeta is a plant that repays regular trimming. As soon as the first flowering is looking a little tired I cut off all the blooms and, working from underneath, remove all the old stems. The plant starts again from the centre and sends out new sprays of filmy blue flowers. The only time when one should not be drastic with nepeta is in the late autumn. When the final trimming takes place it is important to leave an inch or two of stalk above the crown. If you cut it right down to ground level corpses and not plants will greet your sorrowing eyes in the spring.

Irises should be trimmed after they have finished flowering. Some people seem to think that this is a mistake. The experts agree that the right procedure is to cut the leaves to about six inches after flowering. Later on there will be dead outer leaves to be pulled off so that no dead vegetation lies about on the ground to harbour slugs and snails and other creatures.

*Iris stylosa*\* needs drastic grooming. Not only should the foliage be drastically trimmed after flowering but all the brown leaves should be pulled out. I get no pleasure from seeing the flowers peering at me through a tangle of dead leaves, like an old man's blue eyes twinkling through eyebrows as thick as thatch. *Iris stylosa*\* gets very thick, and very untidy, if it is happy. It doesn't like being lifted and divided, in fact it sulks for a couple of years after such treatment, but if all the dead stuff is pulled away quite a bit of the plant comes too and in this way it can be kept to reasonable proportions, and will flower better too. Some of the best *Iris stylosa* I know grow in a Devonshire garden where the foliage receives very firm handling, so firm, in fact, that the flowers always grow well above what is left of their foliage, and look extremely attractive that way.

Some people are unnecessarily sentimental when cutting down their plants. Everything about the plant may be dead except for perhaps one bloom, which isn't quite. They will leave that one bloom, lonely and depressed, goodness knows why because it doesn't look at all nice. It is far better to sacrifice the flower and make a proper job of cutting down the plant.

When dealing with delphiniums and lupins it depends on how cleverly planting has been done whether they are cut right down or only half way. If something else is growing up in front and will soon be in flower the best thing is to cut them down to the ground. In this way a second lot of growth and another crop of flowers will usually be produced. But if there is nothing in front to hide the massacre the best thing is to cut off the flower spikes but leave the foliage for a time to make a nice green bush, but there will be no second blooming.

Like everything else in the garden, deadheading can be done well or badly. With things such as Shasta daisies and heleniums it will be observed that there are side shoots, which will in time produce more flowers, so the stem should be cut off just above the new shoot. Some plants throw up fresh shoots if the old ones are removed from the base directly they have finished flowering. Most erigerons have this happy habit, particularly Mesa Grande, Quakeress and Azureus, so instead of just snipping off the dead blooms get down on your knees and make a proper job of it.

Roses can be pruned at the same time as the flowers are cut. Whether cutting for the house or removing deadheads the procedure is the same, make a sharp, slanting cut just above the first new shoot. There are two very definite schools of thought about rose pruning. The hard school prunes very drastically and there isn't much left of the bushes after they have been pruned in the spring, but it does produce wonderful new growth. The other idea is not to prune at all in the ordinary sense, merely trimming off dead wood. The roses do not make so much new growth, but that will not matter if you have got your bushes the size you want.

Judicious cutting can make quite a difference to the look of a border. With a very large group of, say, Michaelmas daisies, it is not at all a bad idea to cut half the group down to six inches in May. This will mean two flowerings, because the cutting will delay flowering several weeks, and after the first lot have bloomed there will be a second lot to take their place. It is usual to cut the flowers in front, and let them come up to take the place of the ones at the back. If there are a lot of tall heleniums in a border half of them can be cut, and the rest left to flower naturally. Very tall Michaelmas daisies mean a lot of staking, but cut down to six inches in their youth they will never be a problem.

It is very easy to get colours badly mixed, and then the sécateurs should be used to cut off the blooms that are clashing. Shrubs that are growing unevenly should be shaped, and plants that are bent or crooked should have the offending limbs removed.

Yes, a pair of sécateurs is always useful and I envy men their pockets, they can always have a pair tucked away somewhere.

# Watering

Watering was another garden job on which Walter had very strong views. Nothing annoyed him more than to hear that overworked bromide 'You can't start watering unless you go on doing it every day'. His theory was that people who have to go on doing it every day don't water properly. They give a pleasant little sprinkle which damps the ground and makes it smell delicious, without even beginning to get down to the roots of the plants, in fact it tempts the roots to come up to the surface to get a drink, and they get burnt up unless that little sprinkle is repeated every day. If you scratch the ground after a so-called watering you will usually find that the water has hardly penetrated below the surface.

Walter's way of watering was thorough in the extreme. He had lengths of hose with which he could reach every part of the garden, and it took him several days to do the job as he thought it should be done. This, of course, was in the days when one was allowed to use a hose and there was no restriction on watering from main supply.

A sprinkler was permissible on the lawn, but for the borders Walter liked to use a strong jet of water which he directed to the root of every single plant in the borders, and directed it for several minutes.

I can see him now on a hot summer day in an old panama hat and short sleeved shirt, with a tussore waistcoat which he wore for gardening and summer golf (to hide his braces, he always said he hadn't the figure for a belt!). He would stand all day directing the life-giving water to the thirsting plants, with brief intervals for meals. He always maintained that a thorough watering like that would keep everything going for at least a couple of weeks, and he was quite right.

Another theory he repudiated was that one must not water in the sunshine. His reply to that was that it was better to water in sunshine than not at all, because it was obviously impossible to water as he did in the brief evening hours. He was very careful not to direct the water to the flowers and foliage, always aiming at the roots.

I had one complaint about this wholesale watering business and that was that it always brought our persistent clay up to the surface and the next day the top of the beds was solid clay, which baked to iron hardness in the hot sun. I always told him that he invariably chose the moment to water just after I had been round the garden forking up the soil to as fine a tilth as I could achieve. His usual reply was to ask me if I wanted everything in the garden to die of thirst. So, of course, after every great watering I was down on my knees again hammering away at the lumps of clay to break them down and allow air to percolate into the soil. The real disaster was if we had to go away before I had had a chance to get round the garden.

Since the war we have not been allowed to use a hose in the garden, as there always seems to be a water shortage in the summer. Keeping the soil well hoed all the time helps as it allows the dew to get to the roots. Another way of helping your plants to get through a spell of very hot weather is to mulch them. Some people find sawdust satisfactory, manure is good for some things, but grass cuttings are good for everybody. A thin sprinkling of grass will not get very hot but if you are putting on the cuttings with a liberal hand they should be left until all the heat is out of them before being spread round your pet plants. You have only to feel the heat generated in a heap of fresh grass cuttings to visualize what will happen if fresh cuttings are thickly piled round sensitive plants.

Such things as raspberries and phlox, which have roots near the surface, dry out very quickly and are most grateful for a comforting blanket of moist grass. Runner beans get a mulch of about a foot deep. It would be a big job to give runner beans enough water to satisfy them, but by syringeing their leaves and giving a generous mulch to their feet they do very well.

I'd like to mulch the whole garden but as that is impossible I concentrate on the plants that I hope will go on flowering the whole summer. Roses come first, and as I have mostly polyantha type, I do expect them to keep me in colour all through the season. Clematises, if doing well, have a large family to support, so I take good care of them, and remembering the needs of dahlias, I look after them too, but there are only one or two left in the garden which have survived, in spite of my callous way of leaving them in the ground.

Of all the mulching materials I think grass and manure are the best because they get dug into the soil and continue to do good.

# Dahlias

In addition to roses and clematis Walter had a deep passion for dahlias, the bigger, the brighter and the fleshier the better. He bought a large collection from an expert almost as soon as we bought the house, and the first summer they enjoyed a secluded season in front of the hedge that separated us from the next house. There was no other place then in which to grow them, and I thought it was an admirable permanent home for them, a position all to themselves, with a hedge as background, but Walter felt they were being slighted by being put in the background and when I came to plant my terraced garden I was told to leave plenty of large spaces for the dahlias.

Unfortunately they were never labelled, so I had no idea what colours they were. Walter said they were all so lovely that it didn't matter. I held other views but was not clever enough to evolve a way of labelling them. I did try but in the process of lifting the tubers, washing the tubers, drying the tubers, dusting with sulphur the tubers and finally burying the tubers in boxes of ashes the chance of any label remaining attached to the tubers was very remote. The consequence was that I got great blobs of the wrong colour in my carefully planned schemes, which did not endear them to me. They were the most flashy collection of dahlias I have seen, only fit for a circus, as I often told my husband.

When we first started gardening I was only allowed to watch (for future reference) the great ritual of planting dahlias. I think I was permitted to get barrowloads of manure and cans of water, but he would not trust me to do more. In after years, when he could not do the heavy jobs, I had to plant them but he always stood by to see I didn't cheat.

Stock Exchange holidays – the 1st of May and 1st of November – were our aim for the ceremonies of planting and lifting the dahlias.

First of all Walter dug a large and deep hole. He never worried about treading on my plants, or smothering them with the great piles of earth that were thrown up, so I had to be careful not to plant anything within a wide radius. A generous spoonful of manure went into the bottom of the hole, and this was covered with soil. The next job was to ram in an enormous stake which was eventually to support the luxuriant growth of the plant, and then the tuber was lowered reverently into the hole and snuggled up to the stake to make things as easy as possible in later life.

A little 'fancy' soil (I mean for this good compost or a nice potting mixture) was sifted in all round the tuber and then some, but not all, of the earth dug out was put back. Instead of a nice smooth finish there had to be saucer-like hollows to catch the moisture that would come from heaven or the watering can. It was no good for me to tell him that it looked as if the cat had been busy, it didn't matter what my bed looked like so long as each dahlia was given all the comfort that was humanly possible. When he had finished I used to go round removing the surplus earth that was heaped up all round each planting, but I never dared shovel it back into his hollows, as I wanted to do. Some things were sacred.

Watering the dahlias was one of the things I was supposed to do and often shirked. If ever Walter saw me with a can in my hand, giving refreshment to some little stranger, or preparatory to sowing seeds, I knew I should hear 'Are you going to water the dahlias?' I am afraid I got in the habit of doing my watering when he wasn't about. I wouldn't have minded if a small amount of water would have sufficed. Nothing less than a whole canful had to be poured slowly down each horrible little hole – and the contents of one can would bring new life to quite a lot of my small treasures.

Sometimes even the stoutest stake would prove a broken reed and casualties brought gloom into the house. Nowadays, thank goodness, one seldom sees those tall fleshy dahlias, with blooms like soup plates, so heavy that they can hardly hold up their heads. I am glad that the present taste is for less tall, less exuberant dahlias, which are easier to grow and far easier to incorporate into an ordinary garden with pleasant effect.

The problem has been solved for me because I was never very successful in keeping tubers through the winter. Unlike the cottagers, whose favourite place for storing them is in the spare bedroom, I have only outhouses and they are all cold and draughty places. Under the staging of a greenhouse is a good place, but I have no greenhouse, and however carefully I stored them, tucking them up in mountains of straw, the cold always managed to find them and every season there were a few less, until I was reduced to two very ordinary red ones, a double and a single, and these I leave in the ground. They come up year after year and I am quite glad to see them.

# Some Failures

As a gardener I was a great trial to my husband and I marvel now that he was so patient with me. He wanted me to concentrate on the straightforward things like delphiniums and lupins instead of odd things which he thought were not so rewarding. He had little interest in small, unshowy plants that I liked to try, and liked a good return for his money. The only way I could get round this was to keep up the fiction that I did not buy plants and anything new that appeared in the garden had been given to me. It wasn't that he minded the cost, but he took the line that as I did not look after properly the plants that I had (i.e. didn't water the dahlias enough) it was silly to keep getting more plants.

Every gardener knows the fascination of the unknown, and when the ordinary plants are doing nicely there is a great temptation to be a little more venturesome. That is one of the excitements of gardening, but one which my husband did not share. He pretended not to see me with my nose in catalogues night after night, and though I always tried to intercept the postman when I was expecting plants, he always knew.

On the whole I agreed with him that it was silly to try to make things grow that obviously don't like you, certainly not if your soil is wrong for them. But there are some plants that are naturally capricious and unpredictable and it becomes a personal challenge to succeed with them. One such plant is Scotch creeper, or *Tropaeolum speciosum*, to give it its proper name. I knew it could be grown in this part of the world because for several of my friends it ramped away without restraint. But it just wouldn't grow for me, though I tried it in a dozen different places, giving it everything I thought it liked. I planted it on the north side of walls and hedges, so that it could worm its way to the sun, and took endless trouble digging large holes for its reception, and filling them with a mixture of good soil and peat. Sometimes it put its head out to see if it liked the world, decided it didn't and settled down to sulk. Very often it didn't bother to send up a single leaf. Only once did it respond to my overtures but, alas, it had the temerity to choose for its support one of Walter's cherished rambler roses, and the moment when it was ready to open its vivid scarlet blossoms coincided with Walter's decision to cut down the rose and my creeper went with it. Though I continue to struggle never again have I had so much co-operation. There are two places where it comes up most years, although sometimes it will quite happily miss a year or two. It does sometimes achieve a few very meagre flowers at the end of the season, but obviously has no heart in it. The place where it does best now is on a bank facing east, in heavy clay. There is a large double gorse bush growing there and it does make an attempt to climb to the top of the bush, but not with any outstanding success.

Another plant I tried several times was *Delphinium nudicaule*. Once it liked me so well that it produced some fine fat buds, which I watched with daily excitement. Then one day to my horror I found that the whole top of the plant had been sliced off. Walter thought the buds were seed pods, and so off came their heads. When I remonstrated fiercely all the satisfaction I got was that he didn't think much of it anyhow and I'd do much better to stick to ordinary delphiniums!

One thing I never discovered and that was whether he was deliberately trying to teach me to leave experimental gardening alone until I had learnt to grow the ordinary things properly. I assumed that these regrettable incidents were not intentional, but they may have been part of a campaign.

Another thing we didn't agree about was my attempt to have flowers blooming all the year round. He felt very strongly that a good summer garden was what one really wanted, because to him the summer was the time when one enjoyed a garden. He seldom put his nose outside in the winter, and he felt that by filling the garden with things that bloomed early and late I was not leaving enough room for that terrific summer display. I know a lot of people feel the same way, and if I went to Scotland every August I might concentrate on spring and early summer, and if spring was the favoured holiday time make June and July the season of triumph. Since I first made my garden I have given this question of all-the-year-round garden much thought and I have devoted two chapters to the subject. But in those early days Walter thought I was attempting the impossible, and for his sake I had to cram as many of the showy summer flowers into the beds, but I tried to extend the season by planting as much as I could in the walls and between the stones, so that very early in the year aubrietia, alyssum, saxifrages and arabis foamed over the paths and steps. For autumn display Michaelmas daisies met with approval but I was warned not to allow too many yellow flowers to creep into the autumn garden. There was always too much yellow in spring and autumn for Walter and we were always striving for more red and flame in these seasons. Gladioli were the obvious answer in the autumn, but we found them the most ungraceful plants to grow. Of course they should be grown in a kitchen garden for cutting, but we tried them in various places but they were always too stiff to mingle gracefully with a mixed border such as I was trying to achieve. Walter had an idea they could be planted among rose-trees to supply interest when the roses were over, with a ground cover of white alyssum or violas. But it didn't work out as he had hoped, so gladioli were banished from our garden.

# Composting

All this time we were doing our best to improve our terrible clay. We had endless bonfires and Walter tried so hard to get me to take the ash for the garden before rain had had a chance to wash some of its goodness into the soil. I wouldn't admit the necessity. There was always something else more important I wanted to do and it was often a week before I trundled it off to my flower beds. Now, of course, I am as fervent a disciple as Walter ever was. All the wood ash from my open fires is shared among the plants that particularly like potash, magnolias and irises particularly, and I give some to the raspberries, and in the winter the apple trees get their share. When I grew potatoes and tomatoes they, too, were lucky. To distribute it evenly throughout the rest of the garden I now incorporate it in my compost.

Everyone has a theory about composting. I got my recipe from an American book, and I find it works out well. All green stuff is put in a heap to rot down. Perennial weeds and evergreen material are not used, but everything else, including kitchen refuse, grass cuttings, great mountains of nepeta, aubrietia, Michaelmas daisies and all the other herbaceous things that are cut down. For the kitchen refuse I keep a big brown pot (commonly known as 'the gash') on the window sill behind the sink, and into it go all the tea-leaves, apple peels, onion skins and coffee grounds. Also crushed egg shells. Walter made a great fuss about the egg shells, he disliked them so and contended that it was silly to bother about them when I could get all the lime I wanted for a few pence. But I think my plants enjoy a mixed diet and I would not deny them little tit-bits of shell, but I did see that they were crushed very finely so that they did not intrude too forcibly on my lord's eye. I noticed great mounds of coffee grounds at Kew, so I know I am on firm ground there, and as for tea-leaves, you have only to see what emptying the teapot does to a wilting plant. I have known trees and shrubs brought back from the dead by having tea and tea-leaves administered to them after every meal, and I am sure one reason why Madonna lilies thrive in cottage gardens and not in ours is because they get tea and washing up water and all manner of good things given to them. I don't like the messiness of tea-leaves thrown on the flower beds, but I use them and the tea that is left in the teapot in the compost. The liquid is particularly good, in fact a necessity, for in very dry weather the compost heap needs generous watering to speed decay.

I leave this heap until it is quite brown, and then I combine it with other ingredients to stand again. How long one leaves it depends on the speed of decomposition and the supply of material. I have now built up such reserves that the making of the final heap is done in the winter, and the following autumn I have a plentiful supply of super nourishment with which to enrich the garden.

My final heap is made in four layers, repeated until all the material is used up. First there is a generous layer of my rotted compost, then an equal depth of farmyard manure. This is then covered with earth and thickly dusted with wood ash. Pipes are inserted vertically at regular intervals down the heap as it is being built, so that it shall be ventilated. I like to use very young manure so that a high temperature kills any weed seeds that may be lurking in the compost. As my natural soil is clay, and such heavy clay that it doesn't change a bit during its year's sojourn in the heap but comes out a soggy solid mass, like a layer of marzipan in an Easter cake, I am now using sand instead of soil in the heap, but finish with grass tufts skimmed from the vegetable garden. These turned upside down seal the heap and keep in the heat to do its work thoroughly. Very old sawdust can be used instead of sand but it must be well weathered.

No one can call a compost heap beautiful so I hide mine in a discreet little hedged enclosure – our old friend *Lonicera nitida* again. Another enclosure beyond hides a deep pit where I pile oak and beech leaves for leaf mould, a heap of peat mould and the manure heap.

As a lot of the goodness must seep into the ground from my compost heaps I have had the bottom of the compost enclosure concreted. Instead of having the ground quite level it slopes down very slightly, and along the lower side I have about a foot of vertical concrete (breeze blocks in fact). My compost enclosures are at the top of a ditch, so it has been easy for me to run out three small drains into the ditch. The rich ooze from the heaps drains into receptacles placed to receive it and gives me a constant supply of liquid manure. It is wonderful what a fillip this diluted goo water gives to a plant that is just coming into flower. In the summer the sweet corn particularly is the lucky recipient of this largesse.

There is a theory that if compost is made on a concrete base one will be deprived of the worms which would normally come up from the soil. I don't know where the worms come from but my heap is always full of very lively, very pink worms, so I haven't lost these busy little underground workers by working on a clean foundation.

By degrees the soil in the garden is becoming more workable. When we took the house there was only one little patch where the soil was fairly good, and I was told that at one time that end of the house had been a bakery and the baker used to throw out the ash from the faggots he burnt to heat his oven. There must have been plenty of charcoal as well as wood ash to make the soil almost normal, compared with that in the rest of the garden.

Walter used to make me envious by describing the wonderful soil of his garden at Sydenham. After years of working it was fine, rich and dark, and no plant could do anything but its best when invited to reside in it. I used to compare my yellow clay with the soil in gardens that had been gardens for many years, and I never knew why anything ever bloomed for me. They did, and I had surprising results right at the beginning before I became a fussy gardener and took too much trouble.

One of my sisters visiting us during that first summer and seeing flowers blooming in that barren waste airily dismissed the miracle with the remark 'good soil and beginner's luck'. The first statement was not true, although the second was. Undoubtedly there is goodness even in weeping clay, and one may get surprising results from virgin soil, but to go on getting them it is necessary to put in as much as is taken out.

That truism applies equally to the mental as well as the material outlook. Gardening is like everything else in life, you get out of it as much as you put in. No one can make a garden by buying a few packets of seeds or doing an afternoon's weeding. You must love it and then your love will be repaid a thousandfold, as every gardener knows.

I have always felt my family have been very forbearing towards me. Before I was married I didn't do anything in the garden. Every weekend, when my sisters were navvying to make a garden round the little house we built, I sailed off on my bicycle to play golf. And I never stopped saying the most scathing things about gardeners, what fools they were always to be working and never enjoying their gardens, and what was the good of having a lovely garden if you never had time to sit in it and enjoy it? I shall never forget staying with cousins in Cheshire. It was what they call summer in Cheshire, distinctly chilly, and after Sunday lunch we donned our coats and repaired to the garden with books and deck chairs. Very soon I opened a drowsy eye to see my cousin stealing off to attack a distant flower bed with fork and vigour, and I thought she was slightly mad. I was the mad one. I know now that the real enjoyment is in working in one's garden. It is very difficult for a gardener to sit with enjoyment seeing all round him jobs that want doing. I often wonder why some zealous gardening relation did not slay me with fork and spade in my unenlightened years.

# The Value of Evergreens

It took nearly a year to get rid of the pole roses in my terraced garden. We let the house in September 1939 and went to London. Walter became Press Adviser to the Censor and I went with him as his secretary, so it was June 1940 before we saw our garden again.

I think it came as much as a shock to Walter as it did to me. Our tenants were busy on war work and looking after a family in war time. They had done the essentials, such as grass cutting, but the flower garden had received no check or restraint, and it had turned itself into a tropical jungle. The roses had forgotten they were meant to climb up poles, and had sent out long clutching feelers in every direction. An attractive, but particularly invasive, Michaelmas daisy had taken complete control of the garden. This Michaelmas daisy is deceptive. Above ground its fine feathery white flowers are just the foil for stiff flowers such as zinnias and dahlias, but underground its roots run hither and yon like ants from an ant heap. They dash through clumps of other herbaceous plants, entwine themselves round stones and pavings, all the time cover themselves with myriads of shaggy roots which take hold everywhere. My poor garden was a swaying mass of overgrowth. Everything tall had grown taller, nothing had been staked, and the height and untidiness dwarfed the low house below.

It was only a matter of time and extreme ruthlessness to bring some sort of order to the garden again, but when I had done so the resentful roses, now tied back to their poles and having taken their revenge on me by venomous clawings, looked taller and more out of proportion than ever.

Malcolm Keen got rid of the pole roses for me. He first started his campaign by asking if I had ever thought of getting professional advice about the garden from a firm of landscape gardeners. I replied with extreme hauteur that I had not and had no intention of doing so, and closed the subject.

After a few days he opened the attack again. He chose an opportunity when Walter was present and began by a general dissertation on gardens generally and Elizabethan gardens in particular. As he intended he very soon had Walter's interest and was able to enlarge on his subjects. The result was that one happy, triumphant day saw the roses and their beastly poles summarily removed from my garden and planted against the high walls surrounding the garden. Shapely little cypresses (*Chamaecyparis Lawsoniana Fletcheri**) were installed instead.

The improvement was startling, and the effect never ceases to please me. They are just tall and distinct enough to emphasize the curving path as it winds up to the little orchard above, and by judicious pruning have been kept down to the height we originally intended. The nursery who supplied them do this specialists' job every August, sawing off the top of the main stem when necessary and trimming the trees to keep their neat shape of little pointed puddings. The grey-green foliage is a charming foil for the flowers in the borders and I find, with sand and peat added to the soil round them, hardy cyclamen do very well planted under the shelter of their overhanging branches.

The amazing difference those little trees made to my garden brought home to me how important it is to include some evergreen trees or shrubs in any garden scheme. A formal garden calls for formal plantings of clipped shrubs. On each side of steep steps leading to a higher garden a pair of Irish yews give accent and meaning, a low spreading evergreen clothes an awkward corner, and if it is not possible to train climbers up a house tall conifers planted near will be silhouetted against the bare walls. Years ago I visited Princeton University and the only thing I now remember about the buildings is the clever way the foliage trees were used to emphasize the beauty of the buildings.

Most rock gardens are improved by the judicious use of slow-growing dwarf conifers, and in most borders something solid and substantial helps the landscape when there are no flowers. Against my long high wall I have several evergreens, including a variegated euonymus and a choisya, which make a comforting splash of tender green when all is bare.

Hedges have the same effect, and if a garden has definite bone structure of this kind it will keep its character at all times of the year.

When planting shrubs and trees of this kind it is important to remember what size they will eventually reach. When I see a little new garden literally peppered with shrubs that will in time become massive trees I shudder to think of the impenetrable forest that will result. Only a little while ago I saw *Cupressus macrocarpa* planted only a few feet apart in a tiny garden. They were not there as a hedge but as individual trees. *Cupressus macrocarpa* when allowed to grow without restraint becomes a gigantic forest tree with a girth of several yards in its old age. We usually see these trees used as a hedge and then they seldom live long enough to get really big.

# We Made Mistakes

In our endeavours to make the garden more interesting we made every mistake that was possible, and I hate to think of all the hours of work I have put in undoing the result of our labours.

Very early in the game we decided we must develop vistas in the garden to add interest and purpose. In a small garden it is difficult to achieve the unexpected. A big garden gives ample scope with hedges, walls, varying levels and the size of the garden itself. We all know gardens that never achieve character, however much work the owners put into them. We wanted our garden to be 'come hitherish', for just as in a house one should catch a glimpse of something exciting that makes you want to explore further, so a garden should lead you on from one point to another. You mustn't see it all at once, but there must be glimpses that make you wonder what is round the corner.

There were two walls separating us from the orchard, and the higher of these we reduced to a very low level to bring the orchard closer. And then to make the orchard even more part of the garden Walter hatched the idea of making a path right down it to the end. After this was done he said the path must lead to something more than just the end of the orchard, and he suggested a little paved garden with a seat.

So we wheeled down flat stones to pave a circular court, with a low wall round the back and sides. Under instructions I planted a border of tall perennials behind the wall. I used to tease Walter about his 'shrine' or 'grotto' and did everything I could to make it what he felt was needed.

All this time I was buying cheap daffodils for naturalizing and planting them under the apple trees, so there would be something pleasant to look at in the spring when one sauntered down the long walk and took a little rest on the stone seat at the end of it.

But we never did erect the seat, and the shrine very soon became known as the folly, because we quickly discovered that we had not the labour to keep the long walk through the orchard weeded and rolled, and our pathetic little paved garden looked utterly out of place in an orchard. So I was instructed to dismantle it, and in course of time all those carefully laid stones were trundled back for use in some other enterprise.

A ditch made our boundary between our orchard and the next one, and I reclaimed part of it near the malthouse for a small iris garden. It wasn't a vast success either, because it was really too shady for the irises to be baked in the summer so they didn't flower with the enthusiasm they should, but it gave Walter an idea that if we could own all the ditch I could make a water garden. So we bought a strip of the next orchard and acquired a good many more apple trees, the ditch and with it the makings of a wild garden.

This meant a fence as our boundary instead of a ditch, and Walter suggested I should plant a hedge to screen us from the next orchard and tall perennials in front of it. The hedge was very easy, just cuttings of *Lonicera nitida* stuck in at regular intervals, and I divided the clumps of plants from the abandoned shrine to go in front of it.

That again we found was a silly idea. Orchards and flower gardens cannot and should not be combined. It was impossible to keep the flower bed free from orchard weeds and the perennials were soon swamped by nettles, couch grass and docks. So I dug up the long-suffering flowers once more and gave the bed back to the orchard, to which it really belonged.

I continued planting daffodils under the apple trees, acquiring cheap lots when I could, and lifting and dividing those already there. They were a great joy, because daffodils undoubtedly look their best tossing their heads in long grass, but in the end they had to go too. We were faced with the problem of cutting the grass and there again the problem of labour defeated us. We had an Allen scythe, but no one to use it. We begged local farmers to help by cutting it with their big mowing machines in return for the hay, but the orchard had been used for chickens and was so uneven that the blades of the mowing machines were badly damaged. The sensible thing was to wire the orchard and let it for grazing, and that we did. Cows don't eat daffodils unless there is nothing else for them, but they trample them in a heartbreaking way, so that half the buds never had a chance to open. There was nothing else for it but to dig them up and plant them in other parts of the garden. Even if we could have solved the cutting problem and let the grass go for hay it wouldn't have worked. If you take away all the grass you must in fairness give your trees some nourishment in place of it, and the natural way to do this is to offer your hospitality to cows or sheep, who will keep down the grass and leave thank offerings behind.

It was only by chance one day that we discovered that there was a nice stone wall supporting the orchard at the far end. It was completely hidden by a bank. The level of the orchard is several feet above that part of the road, and over many years the earth had sifted down until it had encroached several feet into the road.

The bank all round the orchard was in a deplorable condition, with brambles, docks, nettles and thorns. Nobody had worried about it for many years. With our neat little beech hedge at the top it looked even worse than it was. We both agreed that if we could expose the wall at the end and clean up the bank, level it and plant it with valerian, it would look very nice. The problem, of course, was labour. Walter and the garden boy had other big jobs on hand, and it was considered too much of an undertaking for me.

But in the end I got it done. One of my sisters providentially came for a holiday and helped me clear the weeds from the bank. We had a magnificent time clearing the ground, because there was a lot of bindweed there, as well as the easier weeds. We both agreed that there is no sport in the world that compares with clearing ground of bindweed. It is far more exciting than golf or fishing. Tracing this tenacious creeping Judas of a weed to its source and getting it out without leaving any small broken pieces behind requires skill and patience, and the reward is a barrowload of the obscene twisting white roots and the joy of burning them.

For weeks I wheeled barrowloads of earth along the road, unearthing the wall at one end and improving the bank at the other. In time the finished bank met the clean and self-conscious wall, and I was able to devote myself to the beautifying of both. Hundreds and hundreds of valerian seedlings were planted in the bank and in the wall. For a year or two those in the bank flourished and multiplied, and that bank was a blaze of crimson, white and every shade of pink. But they began to disappear, and now there are hardly any left. We could never fathom the reason why, unless it was that they found the soil that I took from the wall too rich.

We were both very disappointed about this because we admired so much the railway embankments in the district which were ablaze with valerian. The seedlings I planted in the wall never looked back, soon turned themselves into huge plants and raised enormous families. I remove thousands of valerian seedlings from the garden every year and for a long time I hopefully put them in the bank, but now I realize it is a waste of time and I throw them away. Odd daffodil bulbs are now planted there, occasional clumps of tall blue scillas and the wild magenta gladiolus, *G. byzantinus**. They, of course, do not give colour all the year as the valerian would have done.

We tried very hard to keep the grass verges round the house nicely shaven, but again we discovered that gardens and farming don't mix. Cows come down the road twice a day, and can you blame them if they prefer soft grass to the hard road? In damp weather they reduce the verge to a quagmire, and the tractors that park themselves on the other verge make nearly as much havoc. We still run the mower over the grass near the gate and under the wall, but it is not done very regularly as it is really not worth spending much time on it.

On another occasion Walter had an urge to improve the outlook from our dining-room window. There is a rough triangle of grass on the other side of the road, unkempt and full of nettles, and he thought it should be weeded, levelled and kept tidy. We spent quite a long time on it, and there are still a few valerian left from those I was told to plant, but again we realized our folly. That piece of ground belonged to dogs, children, farm vehicles, stray chickens and endless cats, and later to a telephone kiosk and pole. We had no right to interfere; after all we were the interlopers. Anyone who comes to live in a farming community must realize that the work of the land comes before anything else, and I blush when I think of the things we tried to do. The village belongs to the cows and the tractors and you can't turn it into a London park.

But though we weren't very successful in our efforts to take our garden into the road I do admire the people who do. There are certain houses I pass on my various journeys that always make me slow down in admiration. The grass is always nicely cut and the edges neatly trimmed, unlike some places which show a dishevelled face to the road, with nettles and shaggy grass, or brambles sprouting from the bottom of their boundary walls.

# The Water Garden

When we bought the house our boundary, the ditch, was always full of water, and we bought the strip of the next orchard with the idea of making a wild garden, with water running through it. The banks on both sides were to be tamed and planted, leaving the willows just as they had been when the ditch was purely utilitarian. But again we were disappointed, because as soon as we had widened the bottom of the ditch, and had put down flat stones to make pools and waterfalls, the water disappeared. We never discovered why, because both orchards drained into the ditch, and there is never any shortage of rain in this part of the world. We could only think a new and deeper well had been dug somewhere in the neighbourhood, but gone it had, and now the only time there is water in the ditch is after unusually heavy rain.

My friends are more worried about the disappearance of the stream than I am. They seem to think it will miraculously reappear one day and I am often asked if the water has come back. The absence of water makes it easier to work in the ditch, and I spend a lot of time there. The bank facing east is now made into a series of pockets with lumps of hamstone, and here I grow my primroses and rare polyanthus. Half the opposite side is given up to alpine strawberries, and in the other half I have scooped out all the clay and made a peat garden. It is really easier not to have to bother about gum-boots when I want to work here, but I must say that I should like above all things to have a little running stream somewhere in the garden. Water is so companionable, and though I grow my Asiatic primulas quite well under the trees, with plenty of humus in the soil, there is no comparison with them and the wonderful effect of those grown beside water.

At the back of the malthouse the original boundary turned sharply at right angles for the water to drain away at the far side of the garden. A willow was growing crookedly over what should have been water, and it seemed an ideal corner for more stonework. We terraced the ground and made shallow steps down to the stream, and on the other side a little paved court and steep steps up to the orchard. Round the corner we scooped out a lot of the clay and made a wide paved walk with hamstone tiles.

Primulas, *Iris Kaempferi*\* and *Meconopsis Baileyi*\* were induced to grow against the wall that supported the garden above, and on the orchard side I used large stones in the steep bank, and planted such sun-loving things as zauschneria, sternbergia, rock roses and androsace. Walter spent a lot of time constructing a waterfall down the steepest part. He put drainage pipes across the orchard and arranged big stones over which the water was going to tumble to the stream below. Everything was there except the water, and the only waterfall we ever had was the rain splashing down.

We always referred to this little bit of the garden as the Lido, but it was not easy to explain why when no cooling waters washed its shores.

In the end I planted Asiatic primulas in what should have been the bed of our river. It seemed a pity to waste a position so admirably suited to their taste, so I dug out the heavy clay and filled the channel with a good mixture of leaf mould, sand and compost and here the Bartleys, the Postfords, the Millars and their foreign relations enjoy life, with their feet in deep damp earth and their heads in the sun.

# Rock Gardening

Our garden did not lend itself to a rock garden, as such, in fact I think very few gardens do. A rock garden, to be really convincing, must look as if the stratas of rock were really part of the ground, and it must be on a big scale. At Forde Abbey, near Chard, a delightful rock garden winds up through high banks, with enormous rocks that look right. The rock gardens at Wisley, Kew and Edinburgh are equally generous, but unless one has a natural outcrop of rock or a very deep dell or very high bank which will accommodate really large lumps of rock, I think rock gardening should be done in less orthodox ways. There is nothing more depressing than a few stones rising self-consciously from a suburban lawn, which is almost as bad as those dreadful Victorian 'rockeries', which were nothing but a collection of horrible burrs or lumps of concrete huddled together in a shady, dank corner, where nothing but ferns would thrive.

With all our stones it was inevitable that my mind should turn very quickly to rock plants. The first home for alpine treasures was expedient rather than intentional, the two rocky beds against the walls of the barton. The second was also forced upon me rather than of my own choosing. The 'Coliseum' came into being because we had to dig out the soil that had silted down to the west end of the house. When we first came to live here we couldn't understand why that end of the house was always so cold and damp, with a strange vault-like smell. It was some time before we realized that about six feet of the wall outside was receiving the clammy embrace of weeping clay.

On digging out the clay we discovered the remains of an enormous fireplace behind the present chimney. This solved the problem of how to support the ground, which was several feet above the level of the foundations. On each side of the fireplace we made a series of steps from our plentiful supply of stones, hence the descriptive label.

I was instructed to plant what I could between the stones, to relieve the hard angular lines. At that time it was literally a case of making bricks without straw as I had practically nothing to use. Looking round the garden I came upon some stonecrop and pounced on it as an answer to prayer. There wasn't very much and I broke it into small pieces and poked them between the stones. I had no idea that when it settles down in a place it not only starts raising a family but goes in for founding a dynasty as well. I think its name is *Sedum spurium* and it is the most inveterate invader I have ever met. Sometimes in the summer my heart softens when I see its really pretty flat pink rosettes, but most of the time it is war. Its round brown stems creep down walls, intertwine themselves in its classier neighbours, push under stones and across paths, taking possession with grim determination. If, by an oversight, it is allowed to stay on a piece of a flower bed for more than a minute, in two minutes that flower bed will be a solid mat of stonecrop of a particularly luxuriant quality. Every year I pull out barrowloads of it and I know I shall continue to do so until I die.

Perhaps an even greater error was the introduction of helxine*, popularly called 'Mind your own business', why I cannot think, because that is the one thing it does not do. I had often seen it bubbling out of pots in cottage windows, and when I saw it spilling out of a broken-down greenhouse of an empty house I thought how pretty and green it was, and how nicely it would help me to soften the grim stones of the old fireplace and the Coliseum. So when a friend offered me some I accepted it with great enthusiasm. She brought it to me in a roll, like a piece of carpet, and I carefully broke it into hundreds of little pieces, tucking them in with love, and watering them with care, and looked forward to a nice little green line between my stones. Helxine* is more attractive to look at than stonecrop, except that it does not flower, at least not visibly, but it is even more affectionate. Again I know that I shall be scrapping it from my beds and from under stones for the rest of my days. I tried to cover the top of the old fireplace with this busy little carpeter, but it does not care to come out in the open. Up the sides as much as you like, and everywhere else where it is damp and moist, but not where I most wanted it. Later I used creeping thymes to cover the unsightly broken wall. They like to be hot and dry, and will clamber about in the sun most obligingly.

After I had made the terraced garden I had more walls to play with than I knew what to do with. I grew aubrietia from seed, all kinds of arabis, including the double variety and shades of pink and rose, also *Arabis blepharophylla*, which one so seldom sees, but which is an excellent wall plant with its tight rosettes of deep green leaves and stiff heads of magenta flowers. One plant of *Dianthus caesius** gave me innumerable cuttings, and all the rock campanulas were used *ad infinitum*. Saxifrages were stuffed into crannies, in some places I planted gypsophila to foam over the stones, in another *Saponaria ocymoides*. The trailing *Geranium Traversii**, Pritchard's var., is good on a high wall, as it is generous with its trails, while *Geranium sanguineum lancastriense** can be used on top of a wall or in a rock crevice.

The rough wall we made round the lawn was another place where I could grow rock plants. Rock roses and androsaces, aethionemas and shrubby thymes thrive in that wall. I grow great mounds of alyssum, more of the lemon-coloured variety than the golden, here and there a small lavender or silver plant such as *Helichrysum plicatum*, and the green leaved *Dianthus multiflorus**, with its bright cerise flowers, and the salmon pink version, Emil Pare*. The perennial cheiranthus and erysimums are excellent plants to choose for a wall like this, as they are mostly low-growing, and sit down and spread themselves most satisfactorily. *C.* Harpur Crewe is better as a border plant as it makes itself into rather a big bush, and gets blown about in the wind, but *C. alpinus** Moonlight* and *mutabilis**, and *Erysimum capitata** and Rufus are most obliging.

Creeping thymes soon cover flat surfaces, and *Thymus micans** works its happy way up the vertical sides of the stones. Erinus seeds itself, and its neat little rosettes covered with white, pink or crimson are most endearing. I am not superior to *Erigeron mucronatus**, with its smother of pink and white daisies over such a long period, and I love *Dryas octopetala*, with its creamy flowers and oak leaves, which just pour down in a regular cascade of foliage.

It isn't only rock plants that grow in walls. *Campanula pyramidalis* loves to grow in a wall crevice, in fact prefers it to a bed. I have seen aloes growing happily between stones in a wall, and I think nepeta looks better in a wall than anywhere. I put it in my walls, on top of walls, at the edge of supporting walls and at the bottom of walls that rise from paving so that the haze of blue remedies the cold effect of so much stone.

Small primulas and primroses tucked in between the stones at the bottom of a wall are attractive. *P.* Wanda grown like a chain between stones is quite another plant from the bird-pecked horror spaced out at regular intervals between tulips or forget-me-nots. Such little dears as Kinlough Beauty, E. R. Janes and Jill look lovely shyly peeping from under a wall, and where there are big gaps a good clump of polyanthus looks more at home than it does in a formal scheme.

Another good place for rock plants is between the mowing stones that separate the lawn from the wall border. I put large flat pieces of hamstone at the edge of the lawn with the straight edges against the grass and the irregular sides against the bed. Rock phlox and silenes are very happy between the stones, and so is the dwarf iris, *I. chamaeiris**, in many colours. Double *Lychnis Viscaria* is not a real rock plant but it wedges itself in between the stones and provides a vivid splash of cerise against paler flowers. *Convolvulus mauritanicus** is starred with bright blue flowers on a mat of brilliant green until November, and *Scabiosa parnassiaifolia** makes a hump of very soft green with flowers of sad, pale pink.

To induce plants to grow in an old wall the best way is to choose a damp day, then find a good crevice and scratch out as much mortar as possible. Stuff the hole with damp humus, such as well decayed manure or some compost, and see that there are no air pockets. The smaller the plant the happier it will be, because its roots should be enclosed in a ball of earth before it is pressed into the crevice. To keep the soil moist I cover the whole with damp moss, and if the weather turns warm suddenly keep it watered with a syringe. Sometimes one can wedge a stone over the crevice to keep in the moisture.

Planting in a supporting wall should be done while the wall is being built, if possible, so that the roots can be firmly planted in the soil behind. The wall should slope slightly backwards and at intervals an extra large stone should be pressed back into the soil behind to anchor the structure.

A dividing wall made without cement should be slightly narrower at the top than at the base. Great care must be taken to see that there are no air pockets and the earth must be rammed in with great perseverance at each stage. Again, a large stone, the width of the wall, should be introduced at intervals to make it stronger. A foot or a foot and a half is the best height for such a dry wall.

Some people like to make a double wall, say as a front garden boundary, and for this two narrow cemented walls are made with earth between them. Drainage is important and as well as a deep layer of clinkers at the bottom it is a good idea to put in small agricultural drains about a foot from the top. There should be gaps between the drains, and they should be surrounded with gravel. At one end there should be an inlet so that a hose can carry water through them, because plants in a double wall such as this dry out very quickly. Dwarf polyantha roses are often grown in such a wall, with trailing alpines falling down the outside of the wall. Geraniums give a long season of bloom and these again can be chosen to fall over the edge of the wall.

# The Paved Garden

The only garden in front of the house was a narrow strip filling in the space made by the L of the house. When we bought the house it was a forest of rusty laurels, and the earth was so heavy and dead that even they showed no enthusiasm. High humpy beds were banked half way up the walls.

We dug out the laurels and levelled the ground and laid crazy paving. It was our first attempt at paving and it wasn't a good job. The ground wasn't as perfectly level as it should be for crazy paving, we left cracks between the stones which were much too wide, and we didn't anchor the stones with joggles of concrete.

I planted everything I could between the stones but not nearly enough to deter the weeds. The uneven stones became covered with earth that was washed up, and encouraged more weeds.

Walter decided it must all come up and be freshly laid in concrete. I was to be allowed a few, but very few, holes in which to grow suitable plants but there were to be no crevices. Alas, greed was my undoing. I stood over the labourer who was doing the job and indicated which spaces I wished left. There were a lot of them and it brought my husband's wrath down upon my head so that nearly all of them had to be filled up.

The finished garden was certainly neat, far too neat. We used blue-stone for this paving and it is a cold stone, unlike our lovely honey-coloured hamstone. When we paved the garden it was very early in our gardening life and we hadn't realized the possibilities of hamstone for paving.

I did what I could with the narrow beds under the walls, and planted valerian on top of the walls and colourful alpines in the walls themselves, hoping to get a little colour that way, but it remained cheerless and dull.

Luckily for me war-time materials were very poor and the concrete between the stones soon deteriorated, urged on by unofficial help from a crowbar and hammer, and by degrees I was able to sneak a few more living things into that cheerless scene.

I used all the creeping thymes I could get – *Thymus serpyllum* Annie Hall, *alba*\*, Pink Chintz and *coccineus*\*, *Thymus lanuginosus*\* making great grey woolly mats, and an occasional hump of *T. ericaefolius*\* in bronze.

The many varieties of the little iris – *I. chamaeiris*\* – are determined plants and will get the better of poor concrete, and most weeds. The Bride\* is white, and taller than the blue, purple and primrose shades. *Sisyrinchium Bermudiana*\* has dainty grass-like foliage and flowers over a long period. The yellow variety, *S. convolutum*, is slightly taller. Both of them are inveterate seeders and will appear in the tiniest crevice.

*Dianthus deltoides*, the maiden pink, is good for paving as it makes a dark green mat and covers itself with dark crimson flowers over many months. *Dianthus caesius*\*, the lovely Cheddar pink, enjoys a home in limestones and soon spills over quite a large area.

The prostrate veronicas make good floor covering, and in addition to the more usual blue there is *V.* Mrs Holt\*, a delicate pink, and Silver Queen\*, the colour you'd expect from such a name. *V. pectinata rosea*\* has a most attractive foliage in woolly grey-green, with tiny pink speedwell flowers. It looks best when it reaches a good-sized carpet, and this it does in a very short time. *V. amoena* has very fine, almost threadlike foliage, and light blue speedwell flowers.

*Campanula carpatica* is particularly good growing in paving and should be planted at the sides or in the corners of the garden where there is not much traffic. It comes in various shades of blue, as well as purple and white. The three I grow are Isabel, a fine blue, Opal – the most fragile Wedgwood blue, and White Star.

Two good little plants that busy themselves to good effect are *Helichrysum bellidoides*, with tiny ivory everlasting daisies, and *Antennaria dioica alba*\* or *rosea*. The silver foliage of the latter is soon tightly packed between the stones and throws up myriads of little fluffy flower-heads in white or pink.

The aizoon saxifrages are very neat in the way they pack themselves into small spaces but generous when it comes to throwing up a magnificent head of white or pink foamy flowers. Erodiums, either single or double, are ideal for paved gardens, and so is globularia, which, as its name implies, makes a firm mound of very dark green foliage, later to be trimmed with soft blue flowers, rather like a flower trimmed toque. Frankenia has heath-like foliage which turns bronze in the autumn. It makes a heavy mat and is covered with small stemless pink flowers in July and August. The raoulias are arch carpeters. *R. australis*\* is the most popular and rightly so as there is nothing so silvery as the glistening sheet it makes without lifting its head from the stones. The flowers are microscopic, too, yellow and stemless. *R. glabra* makes an emerald carpet with fluffy cream flowers, while *R. lutescens*\* makes the merest film of yellow-green, which turns to silver in the autumn.

The foregoing paving plants do not restrict themselves to the spaces left for them but make big mats covering great surfaces of stone. Other carpeters creep along between the stones, filling all the cracks with greenery but hardly intruding above ground. My favourite is *Mentha Requienii*\*, the tiny creeping mint, with bright green leaves and the tiniest pale mauve flowers. The scent is strong when you press a finger on it, but the time I am most grateful for its fragrance is in the winter, when I brush snow from the paving and the heady scent comes up in waves. I used to think the creeping pennyroyal, *Mentha Pulegium*\*, was as neat and self-effacing as *Mentha Requienii*, but on closer acquaintance I find it likes to spread itself in rather untidy loops and flusters. But its scent is pleasantly pungent and I wouldn't be without it. The acaenas offer new foliage colour, *A. Buchananii** is silvery-grey with yellow burrs, while *A. microphylla* (or *A. inermis*) has bronze fern-like foliage and crimson spiny flowers. *Arenaria balearica* will cover everything in sight when it once gets going. It likes to work in damp shady places and then it gets as busy as helxine*. But no one minds, so fine and bright is the foliage and so star-like are the tiny white flowers with which it smothers itself in April and May. The cotulas are not very exciting but they make tiny lawns of bright green between the stones. Dresden China daisies are still among the best plants for growing in paving. They enjoy the cool root run and increase rapidly, and they never wander beyond their ascribed domain. Their little bright pink flowers are always welcome, and there is a white version called The Pearl, which looks entrancing in a dark corner. The bigger crimson daisy, Rob Roy, I prefer to use in a flower bed, close up against a paved path. It seems a little too fleshy to grow in paving, but in a bed, where it can spread itself, it makes a delightful crimson accent.

It was difficult to decide what to plant in the narrow beds that border the paved garden. Walter planted as many climbing roses as he could clamber over the walls, and we have a fine selection of Paul's Scarlet*, American Pillar and Mme Abel Chatenay, and since his death I have added the lovely white *Clematis Henryi* and the flashy rose and white King George V. Walter and I could never agree about hydrangeas, he liked them blue and for me the pinker they are the better. So I couldn't use these wonderful stand-bys for the narrow beds and had to do with a variation of herbaceous plants, which were never very satisfactory. There isn't enough room to have a selection that will give flowers over the whole season and Walter was never pleased with my efforts. Sometimes I eked out with such stalwart annuals as zinnias and antirrhinums, and we had small dahlias one year, but the blatant American Pillar rose made colour harmonies extremely difficult.

Now I have fallen back on hydrangeas, from the palest pink to deep rose. Nepeta is planted at the edge of the beds so that it spills over the stones, and I am by degrees inducing it to grow out of the wall too.

A few penstemons fill in odd gaps and I find these beds an ideal place to grow *Helleborus orientalis* and *H. foetidus*, as they flower when everything else is dormant.

In the north-east corner of the garden I planted *Hydrangea Mariesii*\* and it has been a wonderful success, giving enormous blooms until very late in the year. *Helleborus corsicus*\* does magnificently in this shady corner too, and its great trusses of green flowers bloom from January to June. *Helleborus viridis* is here too, and a delicious apple pink *H. orientalis* which thrives in the cold, and emerges from snowdrifts unscathed. I wonder why these hellebores are not grown more than they are, they give lovely flowers in all shades from green-tinged white to deep plum, just at the time when one needs flowers most, and the flowers last so long. I can see them from my desk bravely standing up to the worst weather of the winter and I admire their fortitude and grace.

On the south side of the paved garden, near the big chimney, I have beds which house all manner of delicate treasures. Freesias planted in the autumn flower outside in April. Nerines and belladonna lilies bloom in the autumn, and here agapanthus remain all the year round and flower magnificently in the summer. The only uncertainty is *Acidanthera bicolor Murieliae*\*. Sometimes I get a few fragrant blotched blooms before the frost spells doom to my hopes, but many years there is not a single flower. I was told that the way to make them flower was to keep them in a warm place in the winter, so one year I tied them in a paper bag and hung them in the hot air cupboard. A hungry little mouse found them and left me only a few tiny bulblets. I still put them in the warm cupboard in a cardboard box, which I inspect very regularly.

Paved gardens solve a lot of problems and one can make them easy or needing hard work, according to the amount of space allowed between the stones. I know one long wide terrace that is given up entirely to a paved garden, full of delightful things between the stones. It means a lot of regular work to keep it free of weeds and regularly trimmed and tidied, and is not the garden for a busy person, such as a paved patch where the stones are laid entirely in concrete, except for an occasional space. I think paving is very good for a small garden because plants can be put right up against the stones, so that they fall over the paving, and in this way it is possible to get more colour in a small space than with the conventional lawn.

Gardens that have to be left to their own devices, such as the garden of a weekend cottage, always look neat if paving is used instead of grass, and I have known instances where paving is used just as one would use grass, with beds left in it for roses and small shrubs. A very good point about paving is that it is not affected by rain. Beds surrounding a lawn get no attention when the lawn is sodden, but with paving it is possible to go out and work the moment the rain stops.

There are many variations to make paved gardens individual, such as different levels or the introduction of pools and fountains. Walls add interest and here can be used with wonderful effect a lead figure or a sundial or bird bath. Stone urns brimming with flowers help with added colour, or, if there is nothing else, symmetrical bushes or small trees can be used in strategic places.

The shape of the stones used for the paving governs the treatment. With odd-shaped stones, usually known as 'crazy', the planting can be crazy as you like. With large rectangular flagstones the treatment must necessarily be more restrained. But nature is very kind and knows where to waft a stray seed. The severest schemes soon become human with brave little plants poking up here and there. Even at Wisley the humble *Erigeron mucronatus** has the temerity to put itself in a wall, all among its betters!

# The Herb Garden

Everyone would like to have a herb garden – a little oasis of old world plants and delicate fragrance, with clipped hedges of box or lavender, rosemary or santolina. But it needs a big garden to allow space for such a pleasant corner, and someone with plenty of time, for such a garden, like a Victorian posy, must be kept very trim to be effective.

Even without a herb garden herbs seem to lend themselves to original treatment. I have heard of people putting down an old cartwheel and putting different herbs between the spokes, and sometimes ladders are used in the same way in a long narrow space. But I have never known how the herbs were trained to keep in their own little enclosures. Most herbs are rather woody and distinctly unneat in growth. I defy anyone to keep a healthy sage within bounds, and though one might induce parsley, chives or winter savory to stay between bars, tarragon and mint would wander away underground and come up, quite unabashed, in someone else's territory.

Another thing I can never understand is why people grow their herbs such a long way from the kitchen. In the old days when the cook gave her orders to the gardener each morning, it was quite simple for him to bring herbs with the vegetables. But in these days when the harassed housewife does the cooking as well as everything else she hasn't time to go to the vegetable garden every time she wants a sprig of parsley or a pinch of thyme. Some vegetable gardens are quite a long way from the house and when I see in them forests of parsley and great banks of sage, I realize these herbs are so magnificent because they are never used. Knowing how much I resent taking time from the garden to cook, I know I should never use herbs if I had to walk half a mile to collect them.

I grow mine a step from the back door. There was room for a small bed behind the hedge we put in to screen the shameful back premises and Walter agreed with me that this was the place for our herbs. But I grow there only the everyday ones that are used regularly. It is fun to collect herbs but really you can count on the fingers of one hand those that are in constant use.

Parsley, of course, is the first that comes to mind, and it obligingly seeds itself sufficiently for me to find a few new plants to put in when the old ones get too aged. Tarragon I wouldn't be without, the true French tarragon, which can be steeped in wine vinegar for the winter, and is used fresh on steak and to garnish eggs in aspic. Pennyroyal, marjoram and winter savory are collected with parsley for that neat little bunch, a *bouquet garni*, that makes all the difference to oxtail or veal. Chives are in constant demand for cooking with any dish that likes a touch of onion, or chopping over salad, mashed potatoes or cocktail snacks. I used to grow horseradish but it took possession of the bed, and there was no roast beef anyway when we came to live here, so officially it is banished, although it continues to make an occasional apologetic appearance. I grow two kinds of mint, the large-leaved flannel mint for cooking with peas and new potatoes, and ordinary mint for sauce and jelly.

Herbs are most delectable in a savoury butter, to be served with grilled meat or fish, or as a sandwich spread. Being a slapdash cook I choose the quickest way to make it, and that is to cut young sprigs of parsley, some chives and a few leaves of tarragon, and after washing and drying them hold the bunch tightly in my left hand while I cut them very finely with the kitchen scissors on to the butter. After adding a few drops of anchovy essence the whole is blended with a palette knife. To serve with meat or fish the butter is made into pats, which are kept in the refrigerator until wanted.

Caraway is another plant that I allow in the herb garden. It looks like a refined cow parsley, and is a biennial, but one that seeds itself very easily. Seed cake made with the green seeds is sheer ambrosia, if you happen to like seed cake: any seeds that have escaped this fate are harvested and stored for winter use. Most of the other herbs are too decorative to hide behind the hedge.

Rue, with its sharp pungency, must have been popular as a 'strewing herb' in the Elizabethan days, but it really has too definite a flavour for cooking. It is, however, one of the loveliest foliage plants and is a welcome addition to any border. *R.* Jackman's Blue is the best form, with its bushy growth and very pale blue leaves. The pale yellow flowers are quite pleasant, used with the leaves with more distinct yellow flowers. Variegated rue is pleasantly delicate in tone and makes a lovely splash of light in a dark corner.

There are so many salvias that are good border plants that it is difficult to choose among them, but I think *S. Turkestanica** is my favourite. It is such a lovely and dignified plant with its pastel flowers of pink and mauve and its great soft leaves. It is a biennial and produces innumerable progeny every year. But to ensure a succession of plants each year one really needs to start off with two generations, a niece and an aunt, because this salvia usually takes two years to get big enough to flower. *S. virgata nemerosa** (*superba*) has something of the same charm as *S. Turkestanica,* because after the flowers are over the purple flower stems and bracts remain to give colour for a long time. *S. haematodes** has a pleasant loose growth, and makes a good show if it is tied up rather gently before it is too big. *S. argentea* is one of the handsomest of the silver tribe, but it does not care for too much rain on its thick felted leaves and is happier if you can find a corner for it where it can grow vertically, which is not too easy with such a big person. The green culinary sage is such a good evergreen that it should be planted where a hump of foliage is needed, and for this there is a good variety with a purple flower. Good for foliage too is the purple-leaved variety, and the purple variegated with white and pink. To bring sunlight into the scheme there is a soft green sage variegated with gold.

The hyssops make good sturdy bushes that sit down on the beds like a woman curtseying. In the gardens in the barton I have used the blue, white and pink, and in the terraced garden I find a blue hyssop is a good strong subject to grow among fragile herbaceous plants. Unfortunately the hyssops get very woody as they grow older and there comes a time when the old plants have to be scrapped and smaller, newer ones put in place of them. I was delighted to find recently a blue hyssop that keeps small and avoids the gnarled habits of the larger one.

I bought *Angelica Archangelica** with the idea of candying its hollow green stems, or using it like rhubarb for pies. To my shame I have never used it in either way, but I do find it one of the most decorative plants I have in the garden. It has taken possession of the bed behind the hedge, so lavishly does it seed itself. It has to be curbed somewhat but I leave in a double row of plants behind the hedge, where they rise in majesty, with handsome green leaves and great green umbels of flower. Its bone structure is good and it is quite handsome even in death. Flower arrangement enthusiasts are for ever begging for the seed heads. The live flowers have even more charm and every year I put them in a pewter jug in the dining room, where they are a good foil for the oak panelling. Like all hollow-stemmed plants they will last a long time in water if the hollow stems are first filled with water. It is quite easy to manage this by putting one's thumb over the filled stalk and keeping it there until it is under water in the container.

Fennel is another herb that has great beauty of form and foliage and really deserves to be grown alone where its loveliness can be seen properly. From the practical angle I like it because its fern-like foliage, finely chopped, adds a distinctive flavour to salads and sauces for fish, but I grow it mostly because of its wonderful colouring and growth. After a shower of rain a big bush of fennel looks like blue smoke. The stems are smooth grey-green, like young bamboos, and the flowers greenish yellow. Though rather aromatic for a very small room arrangement of fennel and santolina is very pleasant.

The leaves of bergamot are used in *pot pourri*, and the flowers add many lovely colours to the garden. Most people know the scarlet monarda but not so often does one see the white and pink, crimson, lavender and purple. I once saw a whole stand at a Horticultural show devoted to monardas and nothing else, and I was amazed at the number of lovely colours in which it can array itself. The bergamots are very shallow-rooting, and though they like plenty of sun they do not like to get too dry.

Rosemary is another herb that has endless uses. Its informal habit of growth makes it ideal for odd, difficult corners, where something not too definite is required. I like the prostrate variety sprawling over a path, and the erect form – Miss Jessup's Upright – looks well against a stone pedestal or seat. Stoechas lavender is another good plant to grow against stone, particularly round the angular base of a garden ornament, or over steps.

I think most lavenders are worthy of being grown individually instead of being massed in a hedge. A perky little bush of lavender is surprising and pleasant among other shrubs, and an occasional bush among the flowers is very pleasant to meet. Variation can be achieved by using pink, white and deep purple as well as the more usual shades.

Talking of herbs makes one think of bee plants. It is a lovely idea to make a bee garden – a riot of all the plants that bees love best arranged round their hives. Lovely in theory, but difficult in practice, because the bees are so concentrated among the flowers that there is no chance to get near enough to weed or tidy their domain. By all means give them their flowers, but plant them among other things that aren't so irresistible.

# Early and late

Everyone has their own ideas of what they want to grow in a garden. When I started my idea was to make as long a season as possible but I received no encouragement from my husband. Walter was a fair-weather gardener and was not interested in what happened in the winter. He wanted his brave show when the sun was shining and he could enjoy the garden, and during his lifetime I wasn't allowed to plant many out of season plants.

But in the last few years I have found many exciting things to bloom very early in the year, and they can usually be planted so that they are not noticeable among the other flowers in their off season.

The hellebores that do so well in the front garden are planted among the hydrangeas and are quite invisible most of the year, but when they do flower, very early in the year, they have the scene all to themselves. Many people complain that *H. orientalis*, the exquisite Lenten rose, is no good as a picked flower. The secret is to slit their stems up as far as the first leaves, and then they will go on for a very long time. If dejected when first picked they soon revive if put in hot water up to their necks.

I have only one complaint to make about *Helleborus orientalis*, and that is the leaves get so untidy and badly marked long before the flowers are finished. When the leaves are very brown and tattered I remove the worst of them, because no flower, however beautiful, can stand up to a background of shabby, scabby foliage. The hellebores are so beautifully foliaged with tiny leaves near every flower that they can get on very well without their own coarse leaves, when those are no longer worthy of them.

Pulmonarias come very early. Even the ordinary one is very beautiful when nothing else is in bloom, and it is a good idea to plant it where it will not be conspicuous later on, as its large leaves get even larger when it has finished flowering. The less rampant varieties need not be relegated in the same way. The bright blue *Pulmonaria azureus** is lovely in the rock garden, its leaves are never large and disappear completely for most of the year. *P. saccharata rubra* and *P.* Mrs Moon* are both good enough for a front place as their foliage is always attractive.

Iberis, the perennial candytuft, is another early bird, and it has the great advantage of being an evergreen. Its dark foliage makes a welcome change of colour in the scheme, so that it earns its keep even after the starry white flowers are over. I have been rebuffed by more fastidious gardeners because I have large patches of this, to them, rather ordinary plant, but I like its low growth and I am always aiming at clothing my flower beds so that they avoid that naked look in the winter.

Polyanthus and primroses flower very early and I like to tuck as many of them as I can into odd corners, so that their cheerful little faces are waiting to greet me in March and April. Both are so much more effective used like this instead of being regimented in rows or packed together in large areas. Clumps of them among shrubs look lovely, they seem very happy at the bottom of walls and in wall crevices so long as there is enough moist earth to please them. Under hedges and among the taller herbaceous plants they do well, and in any other unexpected place you can think of. I am certain these woodland plants do not enjoy being planted out in full sunlight. I notice that if they have the shade of some tall plant beside them they make much bigger clumps and the flowers are much finer. In the old days there always seemed too many yellow and orange shades in polyanthus, but now there are beautiful pinks and creams and some magnificent blue forms.

Doronicums are very welcome in the early spring, with their bright yellow flowers. There are several varieties, including one very large one which bears magnificent heads on two-foot stems. When these plants have finished flowering we have done with them until the next, so, although their foliage is quite pleasant, I do not allow them a very forward position but plant them far back in the border.

Then there is the elephant saxifrage, which used to be called megasea and is now known as bergenia. The common pink variety sometimes begins to flower in October and November, but is at its best in February. I always look forward to these chubby pink flowers, so closely packed and enchantingly beautiful with their green pistils. The darker-flowered form *B. purpurea**, flowers a little later, and the rich rose red flowers are carried on two-foot red stems. I have a smaller form of bergenia with leaves about two inches across, but it is very loth to flower. Bergenia is a most satisfactory plant, as its foliage is lovely all the year round and particularly beautiful when it turns colour in the autumn. There is nothing more attractive than a large clump of this handsome plant among smaller, less definite plants, and it is ideal for merging a path with an awkward bed. Some people use it most effectively as a border between flower beds. It is very easily controlled by the removal of large fleshy chunks from time to time.

Real spring, summer and early autumn look after themselves, but there will be little left in October and November after the Michaelmas daisies and chrysanthemums have finished unless the gardener gives a little thought to the matter.

This is the time when *Physostegia* Vivid* comes into its own. It often goes on blooming well into November, when its deep orchid flowers have a tropical luxuriance which is rather exotic. It is so sturdy that it needs no staking and lasts well in water. Like many other plants that increase underground it flowers best in rather a constricted area, like a narrow bed beside a path, where it has no temptation to stray and waste its substance on underground roots instead of lovely orchid coloured flowers. I used to think it was called the 'obedient plant' because it grew so straight and gave little trouble, but I have discovered it is because the flowers, which grow in lines up the stalk, can be pushed one way or the other and will obediently stay just where they were moved.

*Verbena venosa*\* blooms spasmodically in the summer but it gets going really well when it is almost time to stop, as if to make up for lost time. It is sometimes thought to be tender but plant it near a stone path, where it can burrow as it likes, and you'll never lose it.

The lucky people who have no lime in their soil can enjoy the autumn gentians. They look best grown in a mass, drifting down beside a path or in very large pockets of rock garden. *G. sino-ornata* is the most popular. *G. Macaulayi*\* is a near favourite, with rather lighter blue flowers, but I find *G.* Kidbrook Seedling\* the most generous of the lot, and the one that goes on blooming longest, sometimes to December. *G.* Inverleith Seedling\* has dazzling blue flowers but they are carried on such long stems and the foliage on the stems is inclined to get yellow and brown before the flowers have finished, which destroys much of the beauty of the plant.

Even with lime in the soil it is possible to grow these gentians. It is worth getting a stone trough and filling it with peat and a little sand, or if that is not possible it is quite easy to build a container with stones concreted together, especially if there is a convenient wall to make one side. They can be grown in the same way on a plateau in the rock garden, or on a raised bed made with peat blocks.

Most polygonums are so enthusiastic that they become a nuisance. But there are two late flowering varieties that do not ramble very much. *P. vaccinifolium*\* has tiny green leaves and clear pink flowers. *P. affine*\* is bigger, with coral spikes and leathery leaves that turn bronze in the autumn.

*Serratula Shawii*\* is not a plant that would draw many cries of delight in midsummer, when there are so many more arresting flowers in bloom, but it is very pleasant to meet a clump of it in full bloom in November. The flowers are rather small, shaggy pink-mauve which look like a cross between a cornflower and a small thistle. Its foliage is daintily in keeping and it usually grows about one and a half to two feet.

The cerasostigmas give their lovely blue flowers quite late in the year and are good value even after flowering, when the foliage turns a glowing red.

*C. plumbaginoides* is a front of the border plant but will grow anywhere, sometimes a little embarrassingly as it is inclined to usurp other people's territory. The less busy *C. Willmottianum*\* is happiest with a southern aspect.

I always enjoy *Aster Pappei*\* on crisp autumn days. Its little kingfisher-blue flowers are so friendly and brave – until the frost comes and daunts them. But one can always dig the plants up before that happens and let them go on flowering away in a cold greenhouse. It is safest to take cuttings every year to make certain of a plentiful supply of plants the following season. *Agathaea coelestis*\*, with its broader leaves of darker green, is a very close friend of *Aster Pappei* and likes being treated in the same way. Another little daisy that blooms late in the autumn is *Aster hirsutus*\*, sometimes known as *Agathaea hirsutus*. It is a South African and grows rather like *Agathaea coelestis*\*, with a hazy mass of trailing stems, but the daisies are rather bigger and pale blue.

For years *Convolvulus Cneorum*\* has had the unenviable reputation of being difficult and not quite hardy, but in point of fact it is quite amenable if planted away from draughts and with a wall or other protection behind it. It prefers to face south and then will weather the severest weather. Its grey satin foliage is always lovely and gives its pink buds and creamy white flowers until November. Its lowly relation, *C. mauritanicus*\*, also likes to flower late in the year. Once established it soon makes a large mat, which spreads over paving or falls over walls covering itself with vivid blue flowers, like inverted limpets. In very severe weather it is not quite trustworthy. Sometimes you think it has succumbed but a little later a few tiny leaves will appear. To save heart-burnings it is a good idea to put a little protective material, like bracken or straw, over it in hard frost.

No garden should be without *Salvia uliginosa* or *S. azurea*. When most of the other flowers in the border are calling it a day these lovely creatures will produce their swaying heads of intense blue high above their dying compatriots. Those tender shrubby salvias, *S. Grahamii** and *S. Greggii**, will go on blooming till frost puts an end to their succession of bright crimson flowers, but one must find a very sheltered niche for them.

Belladonna lilies and nerines come in September and October and go on flowering till mid-November. They love a southern aspect, and nerines do best if planted about ten to twelve inches deep. For me they flower more consistently than the lilies, who sometimes sulk for a year, then relent and push up their very naked buds, without a vestige of green clothing, when you least expect them.

Sternbergias, the yellow crocus that blooms in mid-October, is very adaptable and will grow anywhere. Its glistening yellow flowers cheer me for a whole day when I see them so late in the year. And to make their blooming even later you can dig up some of the clumps in summer. The process of dividing and replanting gives them a slight setback and they'll show their displeasure by delaying flowering for a week or two.

Against a south wall I have a clump of Tulbaghia violacea and find its heads of mauve keep opening till late November. Looking like an allium and smelling like an allium it does everything that an allium does except that it flowers in the autumn.

But the autumn queen to my mind is the Kaffir lily, schizostylis to give it its proper name. It seems almost indecent to bring in bunches of their scarlet or pink blooms to rooms bright with firelight. But these lovely flowers, which look rather like miniature gladioli, last well in water, and continue opening their buds. The first to flower is *S. coccineus*, and you may find the first flower in September. There is a much sought after giant form of *S. coccineus*, and another red, more starry in flower and more carmine in colour, is named after Professor Barnard. Mrs Hegarty flowers next, and her beautiful deep shell-pink flowers are more rounded than the others. Viscountess Byng, who flowers last, is the most robust of the tribe, with longer flower spikes and long narrow flowers like pink satin. I have seen a great bowl of these flowers picked on Christmas Day.

Kaffir lilies like a good rich diet, they like plenty of moisture and enjoy sunshine. If happy they increase very rapidly, and seem to like being divided regularly. I have noticed that those in a sheltered position bloom first, and now I plant some roots of Viscountess Byng in a deep trench and cover them with barn cloches to protect those delicate blooms from winter rain.

Schizostylis always give me a thrill especially when I meet them in an unexpected place. The magnificent blooms of *S. coccineus* in the garden of an Exmoor manor house were to me far more exciting than the meet that was being held there. I found some coyly peeping from a hedge in a cottage in North Devon where we went for tea, but the greatest surprise of all was a great long bed of them in a Cornish churchyard. The church of Morwenstow is imposing and its churchyard quite big for such a tiny hamlet. The day we saw them was bleak and wet in mid-October but that blaze of scarlet lit up the sombre churchyard. I wondered who had planted them and who tends them now. That they were loved was obvious by the generous offerings of cow manure all through the beds, and that they were happy was plain for the wealth of bloom. I wouldn't have said they were growing in ideal conditions, with great yew trees nearby, but their long bed had perhaps a slight tilt to the south, all among the graves, and perhaps they had found something else they liked.

A friend of mine is experimenting in growing Kaffir lilies so near a pond as to be practically in the water. So far the results have been worth the gamble as some of the spikes have opened to the last tiny bud, something which never happens in the ordinary way.

Among the shrubs that prolong the season, I would place first *Veronica* Bowles var.* It is a tiny little shrub, with tiny leaves, so it can be used almost anywhere. Its flowers look like soft blue lace from a distance, and cover the plant with a soft haze. It is worth looking at them closely because though so tiny they are most exquisitely formed. As you might expect *V.* Autumn Glory* comes into its own in October and November, and a smaller, neater bush, with the same late habit, is *V.* Blue Gem*. Its foliage is only faintly bronze and the flowers are lighter in colour than those of *V.* Autumn Glory. Another veronica for this time of year is *V.* Warley Rose*. Rather bigger than the others it is looser in growth and has larger flower spikes of clear pink, most generously given. But it is not so hardy as the other two.

Some of the olearias bloom late. *O. olearifolia** has grey-green leaves, lined with silver, that remind one of the olive, and it smothers itself with small white daisies. I never cut them off because they turn into balls of ivory fluff and stay that way all through the winter.

I don't know if mine is an exception but the *Coronilla glaucum** that sits at the top of the rock garden near the big gate and leans against the south wall behind it never stops blooming. It goes into an absolute frenzy when it ought to be settling down for a winter and smothers itself with little yellow pea-like blossoms.

I expect there are plenty more plants that can be found to make the spring begin earlier and the autumn last longer.

# Mixed borders

Owners of very big gardens have infinite scope for segregating different species – if they want to. I shouldn't, because I like every part of the garden to be interesting at every time of year.

No one can deny that an iris garden in full flower is lovely, but the foliage of irises is so beautiful at all times that a clump here and there among other plants is a great help in creating a harmonious planting. Irises are excellent with other plants in a small stone formal garden and I feel some of their charm is lost when they are planted in a mass.

A garden or border entirely filled with Michaelmas daisies is lovely in the autumn but exceedingly dull during the rest of the year. Michaelmas daisies are a great help to make the average garden bright and interesting in the autumn and I don't know how people manage without them for late summer displays. They come in so many colours, heights and habits that there is always one for every bare spot in the scheme, and it seems a waste to lump them all together, so that they detract from each other's loveliness.

White borders and white gardens are lovely and if there is enough room to indulge in such delights I am all for it. The beautiful silver and white garden at Sissinghurst is a delight, and there is nothing more beautiful than white and silver plants against sombre old walls, such as courtyards and priory gardens. A gold and silver border is another luxury for the over-gardened, and one could have great fun finding just the right plants for it, but for most of us white and silver and gold must be woven into the tapestry of just one garden.

I have never been able to work up much enthusiasm for rose gardens, as such, as there always seems to be something artificial and stilted about them. The happiest rose garden I have ever seen is at Cranbourne.

Surrounded by lovely old pink brick walls the roses are grown in rather narrow beds with little brick paths between them, and instead of the usual, formal raised beds, here the roses are grown practically level with the paths. When I saw them they were cosily muffled in the straw from generous mulchings of farmyard manure, and I have never seen roses looking more satisfied and comfortable.

Roses in a large bed always look self-conscious to me. Some people try underplanting in a rose garden but that doesn't quite solve the problem, and the violas or alyssum or lobelias don't really quite do. I think the answer is to grow roses in a mixed border, or informally in an odd border here and there. One way of getting colour in one part of the border for a long time is to group together several bushes of one of the polyantha roses. Frensham is to my mind one of the best for a bold display of deep colour. Little Dorrit is good for a position near the front, being low and spreading and a delightful coral pink to blend with lavender or pale blue. Betty Prior is a lively pink and a little taller, the Poulsen family offer infinite scope, and the lovely shell-pink of Break of Day is exquisite in association with *Iris pallida* or nepeta. Ingrid Stenzig has tight little flowers of a very deep pink, which she grows on tall stems in large clusters. She flowers right up to December and is very vigorous and obliging. Another late flowerer is Cocorico, a dazzling scarlet, which is semi-double and has shaggy golden stems.

Old-fashioned and species roses have certainly come back to stay, but I do wish their proud owners would plant them singly and not lump them together like a shrubbery. Planted in a mass they lose all charm and individuality. They just get big and untidy and loll against each other, whereas a single specimen at the back of a border or against a wall is a thing of beauty. Cranbourne also gives me a lesson in how to grow old roses. Here they are planted in a narrow bed in the middle of a long narrow garden, with borders on both sides. There is grass on each side of the old roses and it is pleasant to stroll along and take in their beauty.

My borders combine all aspects of gardening – shrubs, bulbs, foliage plants, even little patches of annuals to fill any bare spaces. Quite unorthodox, perhaps, but being a greedy woman I want something of everything, and in this way there is always something in bloom. My husband deplored this habit of mine, and could not understand the real excitement of finding something unexpected coming into flower when everything else has gone to sleep.

I am lucky in having little walls that not only hold up the flower beds but give me more places in which to plant enchanting little rock creatures to sprawl or foam or cascade over the stones according to their nature. Then there are crevices and odd chinks between the bottom of the walls and the stone paths for coloured primroses and little daisies, even something a little bigger now and again, such as *Teucrium Chamaedrys*, *Geranium Endressii*\* or even nepeta.

In the old days of many gardeners, bulbs were lifted every year after flowering and replanted in the autumn, except, of course, those that were naturalized. Nowadays we haven't labour and in most of our gardens bulbs stay in the ground all the year round and have to take their chance of damage from the gardener's fork.

Tulips are the main bulbs to feature in my borders and they usually appear regularly each year, as I know more or less where I have planted them. Some of the clumps increase quite remarkably, others are not so obliging and for that I blame field mice. I have a very pale yellow which looks lovely anywhere. Then there is Niphetos, a lovely greenish white, and nothing gives me as much pleasure as these stately groups of snowy white flowers. Tulips look best planted in a clump rather close together, so that they come up like a happy family. In time the flowers do tend to get a little smaller, and then it is time to lift and divide the bulbs, and replant them with generous helpings of bonemeal.

*Hyacinthus candicans*\* grouped together in a dark corner bring a welcome patch of light in the late summer. This bulb is often misused. It should always be planted in groups of at least six and never spotted about as single specimens. Like the Bermudian snowdrop and the pale blue camassia, its real home should be among shrubs or in a woodland garden. The deep blue camassia I admit to my garden. It doesn't increase like its pale sister and introduces a wonderful note of intense blue. *Anthericum Liliago** (St Bruno's lily) I am always pleased to meet. It is a dainty little plant for the edge of the path, and does not ramp. But anemones I think should be grown in a bed by themselves as they have an untidy habit of seeding themselves in odd places. In the small beds round shrubs planted in a lawn is, I think, a very good place to grow such things as anemones. They don't get in the way of the shrubs and their only competitors are weeds, which shouldn't be there anyhow.

Nearly all of us introduce a few shrubs into our borders nowadays. They give solidity and permanence, and enhance the beauty of the herbaceous perennials planted round them.

They can be roughly divided into four categories. First there are the evergreen, formal trees, placed in strategic positions to make the bones or structure of the garden, round which the flesh, i.e., the flowers, will be planted.

Then there are the clothing shrubs. I mean by that the informal shrubs that can be planted here and there to avoid that bare, bleak look in the winter, such as a great mound of purple sage or a low dark spread of *Viburnum Davidii**. Grey shrubs come next, phlomis and senecio, santolina and helichrysum, to gentle the landscape and to act as a background for the more vivid colours. And lastly there are the small, graceful shrubs that mingle so happily with all the other plants.

There are two ceanothuses that come into this group, which are particularly good for our purpose – *C.* Chas de Fosse*, so deep a blue as to be almost violet, and the soft pink Marie Simon*. They are dwarf growing and flower in the latter part of the summer.

*Caryopteris clandonensis** is a lovely little shrub that never gets too big, and its silver leaves and blue flowers are something to look forward to in the autumn. The stems are very brittle and it is easy to spoil the look of the bush if it is in a position to get rough treatment. It likes being trained against a wall, and this is a very good way of getting the very best out of it.

*Ceratostigma Willmottianum** is another late flowerer, and though it is not quite hardy it does well in a sheltered position. *Viburnum Davidii** is low and spreading and excellent for the front of the border, or planted to crouch over a wall. *V. fragrans nana** makes a neat little bush and smothers itself all through the winter with its heavenly scented little pink flowers.

There are two osmanthuses which do not grow too big. *O. ilicifolius** has holly-like foliage and flowers in October. *O. Delavayi** has small box-like leaves and tiny scented white flowers in May. The red flowered *Spiraea* Anthony Waterer* grows about three feet high and its foliage changes colour pleasantly as an added attraction.

I am very fond of the variegated form of symphoricarpos. Its delicate gold and green foliage looks lovely among the flowers, and for a pleasant flower arrangement try it with the sour-lemon heads of fennel and the silver and gold of *Helichrysum trilineatum**.

Some of the smaller shrub veronicas are neat and give different colours in evergreen foliage. Two grey-leaved varieties that are about a foot in height are *V. (Hebe) carnosula** and *V. (Hebe) Pageana**, *V.* Autumn Glory* is about two feet and has dark foliage as a foil for its violet-blue flowers. I am very fond of *Veronica (Hebe) cupressoides**, which makes a lovely rounded bush about three feet high and has a delicious scent. The tiny mauve flowers are not important but they add a little quiet interest when they spangle the feathery grey-green foliage.

There are many others, in fact there are so many shrubs that one has to be very firm with oneself not to overdo them. Herbaceous plants are the real mainstay of my borders and my real love but the shrubs are necessary to give that solidity and permanence that makes a good all-the-year garden.

# What Shall I Plant?

When I first started planting my borders my husband's insistence on well-grown plants and my own love of flowers all the year round made me look for two qualities in the plants I chose. I knew I could not stake as much and as individually as Walter thought was necessary so I tried to find as many plants as I could that did not need a great deal of support. And as I planted an all-the-year-round garden I looked for things with as long a season of blooming as possible.

Of course, there are exceptions to these essentials. Delphiniums and lupins are seasonal and brittle, but one can't do without them. A garden couldn't be contemplated without paeonies, which last only a few short weeks and need strong supports, nor would we exchange the short-lived fragrance of lilies for the longevity of less voluptuous plants.

There are some things one must have and, if there are as many of the plants that fall into my category to plant among them, it is easier to keep the garden looking attractive all the time. We all know that line about 'looking nice last week' or 'in two or three weeks' time', but the garden of our ideals should not need apologies, it should look lovely and inviting every day of the year.

I like the things that once they start will go on blooming until the end of the season. Nepeta is an example of what I mean. It begins blooming early in the year and if it is treated properly will go on until frosts come. Proper treatment is trimming off the tired flowers as they finish so that there is a constant succession of new growth. The best way to do this is to work from below. Lift up the lady's skirts and cut all the old growth from underneath. New shoots spring up from the centre of the plant and give a succession of fresh blooms. At the end of the season most of the growth can be cut off but it is wise to leave an inch or so above the crown of the plant to protect it against hard weather. Nepeta is quite hardy if it has this protection but I have known zealous gardeners who have lost all their plants in the winter by cutting them down right to ground level.

The soft haziness of nepeta is particularly good in a garden like mine, where there is a great deal of stone. It blurs hard outlines and planted close up to a stone path will spill happily across it. To me a border of nepeta as a flower bed is rather dull and a waste of good ground, but it looks lovely against a stone house, on top of a wall or foaming from wall crevices. The large variety, Six Hills*, makes a handsome mound in an expanse of paving, and I am fond of filling gaps between tall plants with the large-flowered *N.* Souvenir d'André Chauldron*, quite a distinct form with more upright growth, and a very strong nepeta scent which some people do not care for. *Nepeta nervosa* is different again, with soft blue pointed heads on upright stems. Like the others it blooms over a long period and is a useful little plant in a narrow border, as it is the most compact of the tribe.

Geraniums have all the qualities I look for. The tall *G. armenum*, with its black-eyed flowers of wicked red, has interesting cut foliage and needs no staking. It doesn't bloom for quite such a long time as the low-growing *G. Endressii*, whose grey-green leaves are spangled with dainty salmon pink flowers all summer long. *G. macrorrhizum* grows to about a foot, its leaves are scented and it comes in rosy-purple, white or pink. *G. Reynardii* is less spectacular, perhaps, with its black-etched off-white flowers, but what beauty in the crinkled grey foliage. The trailing *G. Traversii* is lovely falling over a wall. The woolly silver-grey foliage and clean magenta-ish flowers are a happy combination, and happy, too, is the way it continues to flower until late in the season.

Not everyone agrees with me that *Achillea Millefolium* Cerise Queen is worth growing, although it never stops blooming. The complaint is that though it starts as a vigorous crimson it fades to a very sad pink, but it is just that variation in colour that appeals to me as it recalls the fascination of old chintz. It does need a little support, but one operation does for the whole season. Several of my half hoops control a large planting, and before I had them I used to make a cat's cradle affair with green string and short, slender bamboos.

Erigerons are very good value too. True they never give a second time such a riot of bloom as that with which they open their season, but there is a pleasant trickle of flowers all through the year. I enjoy the sometimes despised *E. philadelphicus*, which hangs its buds modestly but lifts up its head to face the sky when they open. The way to grow it, I think, is to plant the clumps close together in a mass, so that they are a haze of soft pink. This erigeron is prone to seed itself rather indiscriminately but an odd clump that comes up in paving or at the edge of the path is usually very welcome.

Of the other erigerons the best-known is probably the pinky-mauve Quakeress, and her white counterpart. There is also Pink Pearl which is less exuberant, Mrs Beale*, *azureus*, *speciocus*, Moerheim Beauty, Beauty of Hale and many others. *E.* Mesa Grande is a great stand-by as she will bloom till November, getting deeper in colour as the season advances. To keep up a generous succession of blooms it pays to cut off the flower stalks near the ground, instead of just snipping off the dead flowers. *E.* Darkest of All* is a lovely newcomer in deep violet, with a greeny-yellow eye, but not quite so lavish with its second thoughts as some of the others. Nor is the salmon, E. B. Ladhams, a regular second bloomer, although one occasionally finds a late flower or two. The rock erigeron, *E. glaucus*, shares the long season habit with its sisters, and is a useful plant when a wall or rock garden pocket calls for something bold and substantial.

Of all the flowers I know I think penstemons fulfil my requirements as well as any. For some reason they had the reputation of being not quite hardy, but I think they have outgrown that libel. You may lose them if you savagely cut them down early in the winter, but if this rite is delayed till all danger of frost is over there is no likelihood of trouble. I agree it is very difficult to restrain one's itching sécateurs when the sun shines and the ragged brown leaves defile the landscape, but it is worth the sacrifice.

When people ask me what they shall plant in a narrow bed in front of a wall or stone balustrading I always suggest penstemons. They provide colour for a very long period and there is nothing lovelier against stone than the nodding bells of lavender and pink, white and crimson. The only attention they require during the flowering season is to have their deadheads removed, they require no staking and are not fastidious as to soil, position or climate. With luck they go on for many years, but there are sometimes casualties, and in time the veterans become unshapely, like the rest of us, so it is well to have a few cuttings in the store cupboard.

Penstemons are very useful for enlivening dull patches in the borders. Some of them will grow tall if given encouragement and they should be planted near the back, where their height will be attractive. The blue *P.* Alice Hindley reaches three feet and the small belled coral *P. isophyllus* grows even taller and is really best trained against a wall. I have seen it growing most attractively against a cottage porch. For a dark corner there is the lovely *P.* Hon. Edith Gibbs, cream flushed with pink.

Some of the smaller-flowered varieties have great charm. My favourite is *P.* Hewell's Pink Bedder, with its graceful branching habit and soft salmon flowers. Its white counterpart is rather more dwarf, and so is *P.* Purple Bedder, a deep violet which is almost iridescent. It is hard to describe the moonstone tints of *P.* Stapleford Gem. I used to call it Moonlight before I discovered its right name, and I have met it as *P.* Sour Grapes.

*P. campanulatus* Evelyn\*, which made its appearance as a rock garden plant a few years ago, is even smaller, but holds its own in a flower bed if planted in a group. Its big brother, *P.* Garnet\*, is a magnificent fellow who turns himself into an enormous bush if left alone to grow fat. The large flowered form of *P. heterophyllus*, with its bronzed leaves, is not fussy about soil, but its more aristocratic relation *P. heterophyllus* True Blue* does not care much for lime, and behaves best in an acid soil. I give her plenty of peat and she responds like a lady.

The real rock garden species can be difficult. Sometimes they will grow in ashes if they refuse all other inducements. There is one exception and that is *P.* Six Hills, which is so anxious to please that it simply smothers itself with translucent blue flowers, and sometimes overdoes it to such an extent that the poor thing dies in giving. But its obliging nature helps when it comes to striking cuttings, so really there is no excuse for losing it.

When it comes to colour schemes in the garden there is one thing to remember and that is that the deeper the colours the more careful must be the planning. We all have our preferences. Mine are for the pastel shades, for with them it is possible to have a riot without disagreement. Pinks, lavenders, soft blues and lilacs, with plenty of cream and white never clash, and for emphasis a great pool of crimson here, some deep blue there, and a touch of violet now and again will carry one through. Orange and strong yellow, the egg yolk variety, I find difficult and there are not enough primrose-coloured flowers for my liking. But some yellow one must have. Have you ever struggled with an elaborate mixed flower arrangement without a touch of yellow and wondered what was wrong? One way to deal with the necessary yellow is to flank it with white; white and yellow live very happily side by side.

Some people segregate delphiniums, but to me they lose half their charm by being so treated. It may be heresy but I find delphiniums grown by themselves cold and rather repelling, just as a flower arrangement of delphiniums by themselves lacks warmth. Very little is needed to work the charm and it is only necessary to see delphiniums mixed with scabious to realize it.

There are some colours that don't fit in anywhere. Very strident orange is one, and sealing wax red another. I tried over the years to place *Lychnis Chalcedonica* (Jerusalem Cross) in pleasing proximity with other plants, but I never succeeded. The poor unsuspecting creature was moved from one position to another until I think in time she'd learn to walk. She was pushed further and further away from the heart of the garden until she landed up where she has now lived for several years – in front of a *Clematis Jackmanii,* almost out of the back gate. She was one of the very few perennials I successfully grew from seed, so I cannot let her go out of the gate and my life altogether.

# Living and Learning

One of the most delightful things about gardening is the freemasonry it gives with other gardeners, and the interest and pleasure all gardeners get by visiting other people's gardens. We all have a lot to learn and in every new garden there is a chance of finding inspiration – new flowers, different arrangement or fresh treatment for old subjects. Even if it is a garden you know by heart there are twelve months in the year and every month means a different garden, and the discovery of things unexpected all the rest of the year.

I have never yet been to a garden that hasn't given me some new ideas, and it is surprising how you find most interesting things in gardens that you wouldn't suspect held any secrets. There was a tiny little slip of a garden in front of a cottage in this village that was full of the lovely *Corydalis solida*, something you normally find only in a connoisseur's garden. Once at a church fête in a rectory garden I came on a large bed of *Penstemon confertus caeruleus*\*.

It was in the garden that friends of mine rented at Charmouth that I first met my treasured othonnopsis, and that one small cutting has made hundreds of plants for me and my friends. Except for that unusual plant the garden was of no interest whatsoever. It was exciting to find that pink charmer, felicia, in another friend's garden and better still when I was offered seedlings of it. Now I have to be rather firm with the lady as she thinks that parts of my garden belong to her and her only, but I'd hate to be without her.

One isn't always lucky enough to get plants but ideas are available for anyone who wants to take them. There is a garden I know nearly as well as my own. One day in the spring I noticed what I thought was a new plant. It was used as an edging and was covered with delicate little pale yellow flowers, on wiry stems. But on enquiry I found it was no newcomer but our old friend epimedium with the foliage cut off. We grow this plant for its lovely leaves and tend to forget how lovely the flowers can be. By the time they come out the foliage is tattered and shabby and it is sensible to remove it so that the full beauty of the flowers and the new leaves, in palest green pink tinged, can have the stage.

In the same garden I realized how kind and softening stoechas lavender can be if planted to blur the hard lines of stonework. Here wide steps led up to a terrace on which is a large stone basin. The lazy growth and hazy colouring of the lavender give a peaceful feeling of permanence and grace. Stonework can be rather uncompromising at times but careful planting humanizes it.

I adopted this idea in my own garden. It was suggested to me that an old stone seat would look right on my terrace, and at the time all I could find for the purpose was an old stone sink. The front part was cut away and it was hoisted on two rather solid blocks of stone, but it looked clumsy and uncouth, and I really couldn't bear to look at it until it was partly hidden by growing things. A huge plant of *Statice latifolia** in the foreground gives bold foliage all the year round and in the summer a cloud of soft blue. Again rosemary has come to the rescue, and a prostrate cupressus makes a swirl of grey-green against the hard stone. A downy mat of *Stachys lanata** is spreading pleasantly towards the seat and, what is even better, I see tiny seedlings appearing in tinier cracks in the paving. Kind nature is doing the job for me, in a gentle haphazard way which is much more pleasing than my more deliberate efforts.

Another gardening friend gave me the idea for one of my most successful plantings. On the left of the little crazy path that leads to the barton the higher ground is held up by a stone wall. At one spot the ground behind is level with the wall, and it was here that I planted a *Cytisus kewensis** to spread across the bed and pour down the wall.

I look forward each year to the moment when that corner becomes a sheet of deep cream, a haze of forget-me-nots nearby and nepeta and roses in the background, all smiling and shining in the spring sunshine. It even excites people who are not gardeners and know nothing about gardening.

The same friend suggested I plant *Euphorbia Wulfenii** in the top terrace, as a screen and for emphasis. Again it was a stroke of genius. Never have I seen this spurge so happy and luxuriant, and in that position none of the beauty of its magnificence is lost.

I could go on and on. But that is just what gardening is, going on and on. My philistine of a husband often told with amusement how a cousin when asked when he expected to finish his garden replied 'Never, I hope'. And that, I think, applies to all true gardeners.

# Plant name changes

In her writings Margery Fish naturally used the plant names that were familiar to her and which were considered acceptable at the time. But times have changed, and while many of the names she used are still current, and many that are not are nevertheless recognisable, some have changed completely.

So to help contemporary gardeners understand exactly which plants Mrs Fish is discussing, we have given the current accepted name alongside the name Mrs Fish used where we feel this is helpful. This has caused problems.

In some cases Mrs Fish gives two different names for the same plant, yet modern thinking may apply these two names to two different entities. She may also give two different names for what she asserts are two different plants yet modern thinking assures us that the two plants are the same. In some cases she indicates that one name has been superseded by another while it may now be clear that the first name, or another name altogether, is actually correct. Occasionally, Mrs Fish uses a name that has never been valid; sometimes it's clear that this is simply a misspelling, sometimes the origin of the mistake is less obvious; a little detective work has usually revealed her intent.

So while acknowledging that an entirely accurate explanation of these nomenclatural niceties would be impossible without many cumbersome footnotes, we hope that our additions will prove helpful. In identifying the correct names we sought advice and clarification from The PlantFinder, a range of modern encyclopedias and monographs together with expert individuals. But Mrs Fish grew such an extraordinary range of plants, some obscure even by today's standards and some now completely lost, that a few minor problems remain unresolved.

In general we have changed Mrs Fish's original text as little as possible but the accepted manner in which names are styled in type has also changed over the years. So in some cases we have simply modified the expression of an otherwise correct name in order to avoid unnecessary additions.

The science of plant nomenclature perhaps should be, but is certainly not, a precise one; however, we feel sure that by making these additions we add to an appreciation of Mrs Fish's writing and of the plants she grew.

*Graham Rice*

| Plant name in the text | Correct current name |
|---|---|
| *Acidanthera bicolor* | *Acaena buchananii* |
| *Acidanthera bicolor Murieliae* | *Gladiolus callianthus* 'Murielae' |
| *Agathaea coelestis* | *Felicia amelloides* |
| *Angelica Archangelica* | *Angelica archangelica* |
| *Antennaria dioica alba* | *Antennaria dioica* 'Alba' |
| *Anthericum Liliago* | *Anthericum liliago* |
| *Aster Pappei* | *Felicia amoena* |
| *Aster hirsutus* | *Felicia hirsuta* |
| *Bergenia purpurea* | *Bergenia cordifolia* 'Purpurea' |
| *Caryopteris clandonensis* | *Caryopteris* × *clandonensis* |
| *Ceanothus* Chas de Fosse | *Ceanothus* 'Charles de Fosse' |
| *Ceanothus* Marie Simon | *Ceanothus* × *pallidus* 'Marie Simon' |
| *Ceanothus Veitchianus* | *Ceanothus* × *veitchianus* |
| *Ceratostigma Willmottianum* | *Ceratostigma willmottianum* |
| *Chamaecyparis Lawsoniana Fletcheri* | *Chamaecyparis lawsoniana* 'Fletcheri' |
| *Cheiranthus alpinus* | *Erysimum hieracifolium* |

| | |
|---|---|
| *Cheiranthus* Moonlight | *Erysimum* 'Moonlight' |
| *Cheiranthus mutabilis* | *Erysimum mutabile* |
| *Chimonanthus fragrans* | *Chimonanths praecox* |
| *Chimonanthus lutea* | *Chimonanths praecox* var. *luteus* |
| *Convolvulus Cneorum* | *Convolvulus cneorum* |
| *Convolvulus mauritanicus* | *Convolvulus sabatius* |
| *Coronilla glaucum* | *Coronilla valentina* subsp. *glauca* |
| *Cytisus kewensis* | *Cytisus* × *kewensis* |
| *Dianthus caesius* | *Dianthus gratianopolitanus* |
| *Dianthus multiflorus* | *Dianthus barbatus* × *D. plumarius* |
| *Dianthus multiflorus* Emil Pare | *Dianthus* Emil Paré |
| *Erigeron* Darkest of All | *Erigeron* 'Dunkelste Aller' |
| *Erigeron* Mrs Beale | *Erigeron* 'Mrs F. H. Beale' |
| *Erigeron mucronatus* | *Erigeron karvinskianus* |
| *Erysimum capitata* | *Erysimum capitatum* |
| *Eucalyptus Gunnii* | *Eucalyptus gunnii* |
| *Euphorbia Wulfenii* | *Euphorbia characias* subsp. *wulfenii* |
| *Gentiana* Inverleith seedling | *Gentiana* 'Inverleith' |
| *Gentiana* Kidbrook seedling | *Gentiana* × *macaulayi* ' Kidbrooke Seedling' |
| *Gentiana* Macaulayi | *Gentiana* × *macaulayi* |
| *Geranium armenum* | *Geranium psilostemon* |
| *Geranium Endressii* | *Geranium endressii* |
| *Geranium Reynardii* | *Geranium renardii* |
| *Geranium sanguineum lancastriense* | *Geranium sanguineum* var. *striatum lancastriense* |
| *Geranium Traversii* | *Geranium traversii* |
| *Gladiolus byzantinus* | *Gladiolus communis* subsp. *byzantinus* |
| *Helichrysum trilineatum* | *Helichrysum splendidum* |
| *Helleborus corsicus* | *Helleborus argutifolius* |
| *Helxine* | *Soleirolia* |

| | |
|---|---|
| *Hyacinthus candicans* | *Galtonia candicans* |
| *Hydrangea Mariesii* | *Hydrangea macrophylla* 'Mariesii' |
| *Iris chamaeiris* | *Iris lutescens* |
| *Iris Kaempferi* | *Iris ensata* |
| *Iris stylosa* | *Iris unguicularis* |
| *Iris* The Bride | *Iris* 'Bride' |
| *Meconopsis Baileyi* | *Meconopsis betonicifolia* |
| *Mentha Pulegium* | *Mentha pulegium* |
| *Mentha Requienii* | *Mentha requienii* |
| *Nepeta* Six Hills | *Nepeta* 'Six Hills Giant' |
| *Nepeta* Souvenir d'André Chauldron | *Nepeta sibirica* 'Souvenir d'André Chaudron' |
| | |
| *Olearia olearifolia* | *Olearia* 'Waikariensis' |
| *Osmanthus Delavayi* | *Osmanthus delavayi* |
| *Osmanthus ilicifolius* | *Osmanthus heterophyllus* |
| *Penstemon campanulatus* Evelyn | *Penstemon* 'Evelyn' |
| *Penstemon confertus caeruleus* | *Penstemon angustifolius* |
| *Penstemon* Garnet | *Penstemon* 'Andenken an Friedrich Hahn' |
| | |
| *Penstemon heterophyllus* True Blue | *Penstemon heterophyllus* |
| *Physostegia Vivid* | *Physostegia virginiana* 'Vivid' |
| *Polygonum affine* | *Persicaria affinis* |
| *Polygonum vaccinifolium* | *Persicaria vaccinifolia* |
| *Pulmonaria azureus* | *Pulmonaria angustifolia* subsp. *azurea* |
| | |
| *Pulmonaria* Mrs Moon | *Pulmonaria saccharata* 'Mrs Moon' |
| *Raoulia australis* | *Raoulia hookeri* |
| *Raoulia lutescens* | *Raoulia australis* Lutescens Group |
| *Rosa Paul's Scarlet* | *Rosa* 'Paul's Scarlet Climber' |
| *Salvia Grahamii* | *Salvia microphylla* var. *microphylla* |
| *Salvia Greggii* | *Salvia greggii* |
| *Salvia haematodes* | *Salvia pratensis* Haematodes Group |

| | |
|---|---|
| *Salvia Turkestanica* | *Salvia sclarea* var. *sclarea* |
| *Salvia virgata nemerosa* | *Salvia nemerosa* |
| *Scabiosa parnassiaefolia* | *Pterocephalus perennis* |
| *Serratula Shawii* | *Serratula seoanei* |
| *Silene Schafta* | *Silene schafta* |
| *Sisyrinchium Bermudiana* | *Sisyrinchium angustifolium* |
| *Spiraea* Anthony Waterer | *Spiraea japonica* 'Anthony Waterer' |
| *Stachys lanata* | *Stachys byzantina* |
| *Statice latifolia* | *Limonium platyphyllum* |
| *Thymus ericaefolius* | *Thymus ericoides* |
| *Thymus lanuginosus* | *Thymus pseudolanuginosus* |
| *Thymus micans* | *Thymus caespititus* |
| *Thymus Serpyllum alba* | *Thymus serpyllum* var. *albus* |
| *Thymus serpyllum coccineus* | *Thymus* 'Coccineus' |
| *Verbena venosa* | *Verbena rigida* |
| *Veronica* Autumn Glory | *Hebe* 'Autumn Glory' |
| *Veronica* Blue Gem | *Hebe* × *franciscana* 'Blue Gem' |
| *Veronica Bowles var.* | *Hebe* 'Bowles Hybrid' |
| *Veronica carnosula* | *Hebe carnosula* |
| *Veronica cupressoides* | *Hebe cupressoides* |
| *Veronica* Mrs Holt | *Veronica prostrata* 'Mrs Holt' |
| *Veronica Pageana* | *Hebe pinguifolia* 'Pagei' |
| *Veronica pectinata rosea* | *Veronica pectinata* 'Rosea' |
| *Veronica* Silver Queen | *Veronica prostrata* 'Silver Queen' |
| *Veronica* Warley Rose | *Hebe* 'Warley Pink' |
| *Viburnum Davidii* | *Viburnum davidii* |
| *Viburnum fragrans nana* | *Viburnum farreri* 'Nanum' |

# Index